Table of Contents

Step 1: Clothing 5

Step 2: Shotguns 9

Step 3: Shotgun Shells and Other Items to Bring Hunting 14

Step 4: Licensing, Hunter Safety and Rules 18

Step 5: Decoy Types 21

Step 6: How to Find the Ducks 37

Step 7: Hunting Crop Fields 40

Step 8: How to Get Permission to Hunt Private Land 42

Step 9: Finding Public Land to Hunt 46

Step 10: The Duck Hunting Season 49

Step 11: Time of Day to Hunt 52

Step 12: Number of Decoys to Use 55

Step 13: Wind Direction 62

Step 14: Impact of Weather 67

Step 15: Concealing Yourself from the Ducks 73

Step 16: Decoy Setup and Adjustment 81

Step 17: Hunting Without Decoys 98

Step 18: Duck Calling 101

Step 19: Other Attention-Grabbing Techniques 104

Step 20: Shooting 108

Step 21: Duck Cleaning 112

Bonus #1 Accelerate Your Duck Hunting Success 116

Bonus #2 Painting and Repairing Decoys 118

Final Words 120

Copyright © 2015 by GuideHunting LLC. All rights reserved.

No part of this book may be reproduced, stored in a retrieval system, or transmitted by any means, electronic, mechanical, photocopying, recording, or otherwise, without written permission from the author.

Are You Ready to Hunt Ducks?

The Key to Duck Hunting Success is Found Right Here in this Book

In this book I teach you all of the essentials you need to know to achieve the best results possible in the sport of duck hunting. It is my goal to save you the pain, heartache and lost time that many hunters experience when they participate in this sport.

Sample Decoy Setup Diagram Included in this Book:

Overview:

- To begin, I will review the equipment you need including decoys, shotguns, clothing and more.

- Next I cover where to hunt, how to get permission to hunt private land, using wind direction to your advantage, and detailed decoy setup instructions.

- The final portion of this book covers shooting techniques and what to do after you shoot.

Attention Duck Hunters...

"Finally, A Comprehensive Resource For Duck Hunting All In One Place. It Has Never Been So Easy To Start Duck Hunting!"

What Are the Common Mistakes Duck Hunters Make?

1. Not properly concealing themselves
2. Using poor shooting techniques
3. Using an ineffective decoy setup

How Do You Avoid These Mistakes?

In this book I will equip you with the knowledge you need to immediately experience success in this sport. Put these lessons into action to avoid or discontinue making the common mistakes.

Who Can Benefit from This Book?

I provide relevant information for duck hunters of any experience level:

- People curious about this sport
- People ready to get started in this sport
- Novice duck hunters
- Duck hunters struggling for success

Now let's get started...

Step 1: Clothing

Proper Dress is Important for Success and Comfort

There is nothing worse than being all set in your hunting spot, ready for a great day of shooting duck, only to become wet or cold. If this happens you will have a miserable hunt or end up having to pack up and head home early. It is important that you are properly dressed to survive the common elements that you will encounter when waterfowl hunting. It is best to make sure all the clothing you purchase for duck hunting is waterproof, not only for hunting over water, but in case you end up hunting in the rain or encountering morning dew.

Here are the items that you will need:

- Camouflage Waterproof Coat
- Camouflage Waterproof Pants
- Waterproof Gloves
- Camouflage Hat / Facemask
- Camouflage Waterproof Knee Boots
- Waders (depending on location of your hunt)

Camouflage Waterproof Coat

When you are duck hunting you will often be in some cold, windy and sometimes wet conditions. I highly recommend that you invest in a camouflage waterproof coat. If you plan to have a long day of exciting hunting you do not want to risk getting wet and being miserable, so be sure you have a coat that will keep you warm and dry.

A coat that is two layers is ideal as it will provide versatility for hunting in different temperatures. If you are hunting the early season you may only need the inner layer to keep warm. As the season progresses a thicker outer shell is nice to have. Also, the layers are nice because they allow for a quick wardrobe adjustment to accommodate the rising temperatures throughout the day.

It is also good to have a hood on your coat. There is a good chance that on at least one of your duck hunting trips you will be hunting in the rain. Rainy days can be some of the best days for duck hunting so a waterproof coat with a hood is key to being comfortable. You can simply pull the hood over your head to help you stay drier on those rainy days.

It is also good to have a lot of pockets in your coat. There are several small items that you will need to carry with you to your hunting spot such as shotgun shells, a flashlight, a hunting knife, and possibly a duck call. A coat with a lot of pockets will make it easier to carry and keep track of these essential hunting items.

Camouflage Waterproof Pants
In addition to the obvious need for these when hunting over water, when you are walking out to your favorite hunting spot you could be brushing against tall grass or plants that are covered with water from the morning dew. This is one reason why it would be beneficial to invest in waterproof pants. Also, many times I actually duck hunt by sitting in the weeds alongside a pond or river. Having good waterproof pants allows me to sit down without

having to worry about getting wet. Of course these would also be invaluable to have for hunting in the rain, which can be a great time to hunt duck, as I will discuss later. Waterproof pants will usually cost between $40-$80 but they are a very worthwhile investment.

Waterproof Gloves

Waterproof gloves are a must for duck hunting. You could potentially spend many hours sitting in the cold or in the rain waiting for ducks to come. It is important to keep your fingers warm and dry so when you do have birds approach you will be ready to take quick action. Ideally, thin yet warm gloves are best as you will stay warm and still be able to get your finger onto the trigger area of your gun.

You could also use hunting gloves that double as mittens. The mitten portion folds back to expose your fingers when you need them, but they keep your fingers warm otherwise. These are an excellent choice to keep you plenty warm while waiting for ducks but also give you quick access to the trigger when ducks come.

Camouflage Hat / Facemask

In the warmer fall days, a camouflage baseball hat is what I use for my duck hunting trips. These hats hide my head well enough so that I am not seen by approaching ducks while still allowing my ears to be exposed so I can listen for ducks without any loss of sound.

When the temperatures dip as the season progresses you will want to convert over to a camouflage stocking hat. They might dampen a little bit of the sound as you try to listen for ducks, but I would rather have that issue than cold ears. Some stocking hats also convert into facemasks which is nice if you are hunting on a very cold day.

Waterproof Knee Boots

Waterproof knee boots are great because most styles are versatile enough to be warm in the cold weather but not too hot on the warmer days. It is good to have waterproof boots in case you go through water or mud. They are usually made out of rubber and extend almost up to your knee.

If you are not going to be entering deep water, knee boots are nice because they allow much more mobility than waders. Waders are certainly a great tool for placing decoys in deep water or retrieving your kill from water that is past your knee, but they are typically not something that you want to wear if you are walking long distances.

In contrast, waterproof knee boots are versatile and quite comfortable. Most styles are slip-on so you just step into them without having to tie any laces. A good pair of waterproof knee boots will start around $80 and go up to about $200. If you are not hunting over water (for instance you are hunting in a field or other dry location) you could probably get away with shorter boots, but if you will be near water at all, it would be best for you to have knee boots.

Waders

Depending on where you are hunting you may need waders. Waders are essentially waterproof pants with a bib and with boots attached to them. When wearing waders you can walk into water up to 3-4 feet deep and stay completely dry. If you are setting up your decoys on the edge of a pond or lake it is great to have waders so you can simply walk in and quickly set up your decoy spread. These also allow you to retrieve any birds that you shoot from the water while staying dry. Another benefit of waders is that they will help keep you very warm. This is because they hold in all of the heat from your feet up to your chest. Sometimes I put on waders even if I am not planning on going in deep water just for the extra warmth.

One thing to mention about putting on waders is that they can cause your pants to ride up inside of the waders because they are tight around your legs. This can make for an uncomfortable experience. When putting on waders it is best to tuck your pants into your socks first so your pants don't bunch up. There is a product on the market called a pant guard which is an elastic band with Velcro on the end that you can use to strap your pants into place. I have personally never used them but it is my opinion that the method of tucking your pants into your socks will be the easiest.

Now let's examine shotguns…

Step 2: Shotguns

What Type of Shotgun Do You Need?

Shotguns are a must for waterfowl hunting. It is my hope that money does not have to be a roadblock to you getting out and enjoying duck hunting so my suggestion is if you can afford a new gun that is great but otherwise starting off with using what you already have or using a borrowed gun is the best way to get started. After time when your budget permits or when you decide you really enjoy the sport then go ahead and spend more on a shotgun. Most any kind can work, but if you have options or are looking to buy a new shotgun here are some considerations.

Shotgun considerations:

- Pump shotguns
- Semi-automatic shotguns

- Gauge options
- Chamber size
- Barrel length

Pump Shotguns

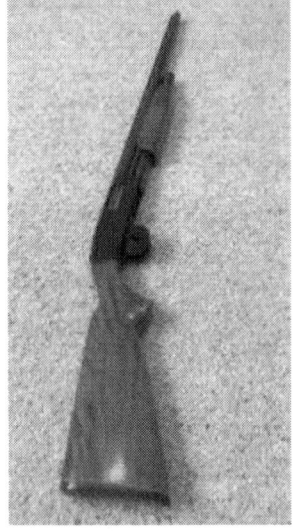

Pump shotguns are one of the most common types of shotguns. This is in part because they are one of the most cost effective shotguns that you can find. You can get a new entry-level pump shotgun for a few hundred dollars. Of course you could spend much more if you wanted a gun with more features or an expensive brand name gun, but that is not necessary.

The basic concept of a pump shotgun is that the gun reloads by a manual action that you make. There is a mechanism called a pump on the barrel of the gun that you pull back towards you each time after you shoot. This action loads the next shell into the chamber and the gun is then ready to take another shot. Because you have to take this action between shots, you cannot take consecutive shots quite as quickly as a semi-auto shotgun which we will discuss shortly, but with practice you will be able to fire shots rapidly.

Pros:

- Costs less than a semi-automatic shotgun
- Easy to find

Cons:

- Somewhat slower rate of fire for consecutive shots due to required pumping action between shots

Semi-Automatic Shotguns

Semi-automatic shotguns are also popular, particularly with people who hunt other waterfowl, such as geese, in addition to ducks. The benefit of semi-automatic shotguns is that there is no action required of the hunter to load the next round into the chamber. As soon as the hunter pulls the trigger to fire a round, the gun automatically loads the next shell into the chamber.

This presents a huge advantage over a pump shotgun when it comes to rate of fire. With semi-automatic shotguns you can shoot several rounds in just a few seconds, increasing your chances of bagging a duck. However, the biggest downside of a semi-automatic shotgun is the cost. Brand new these can start around $500, but in reality the majority of semi-automatic shotguns will be closer to $800 for a very basic model. If you also hunt geese or other waterfowl it might be worth the investment.

The first several years that I hunted ducks I used a pump style shotgun and it worked well. It was actually a gun that my dad had passed down to me and it worked great for many years. However, when the gun started to have a few issues I upgraded to a semi-automatic shotgun. After getting one I understood why they are so popular. Personally, I like that I do not have to worry about pumping another round into the chamber anymore. With the semi-auto I am able to focus all of my efforts on aiming my gun at the ducks and easily take follow up shots if needed.

Pros:

- Fast reloading time
- Do not need to worry about taking any action between shots
- Help keep all of your focus on shooting ducks vs. reloading

Cons:

- High cost
- Not as common so might not be able to borrow one

Gauge Options

With shotguns, the gauge refers to the weight of a solid sphere of lead that will fit the bore of the firearm, and is expressed as the multiplicative inverse of the sphere's weight as a fraction of a pound (e.g., a $\frac{1}{12}$th pound ball fits a 12-gauge bore). Ok, so that is the technical definition and probably a little confusing right? Basically, the lower the gauge size the more powerful the gun. For example, a 20-gauge shotgun is less powerful than a 12-gauge shotgun. The most common gauge options are 20, 16, 12 and 10.

The downside of more powerful shotguns is they have stronger recoil when you shoot them. If you are doing a lot of shooting in a given day your shoulders can get sore from the recoil of each shot. The standard shotgun for waterfowl hunting is a 12-gauge and these are very effective in most situations. If you are a youth or smaller-sized hunter then a 20-gauge shotgun may work best for you. It will not have quite as much power, but it will typically be light enough for the majority of smaller hunters to be able to handle the weight and recoil.

Chamber Size

Chamber size refers to the length of shotgun shell that your gun can hold. I will go more into shell sizes later, but it is important to note that you should find a shotgun with a chamber size of at least 3 inches. This can be as high as 3 ½ inches so if that is available that would work too, as long as it is at least 3 inches. However, the larger-chambered guns usually cost more. Common chamber sizes are 2 1/2, 2 ¾, 3 and 3 ½ inches. Again I would recommend finding a gun with a 3 inch chamber for most duck hunting situations but if a 3 ½ inch is available they can be nice for added versatility.

Barrel Length

The barrel length of a shotgun refers to the length of the barrel that extends beyond the primary workings of the shotgun. Typically longer barrels will keep the shot pattern tighter for further distances. This means that your shots can be effective for longer distances. However, the downside of having a longer barrel length is that it can add weight to your gun and make it more difficult to carry. For example, you will often be walking through woods or tall grass to make it to your hunting location. The longer barrels can make it a little more challenging as you navigate to the hunting spot.

The most common barrel lengths for waterfowl shotguns are 26, 28 and 30 inches. My preference is a 28-inch barrel as it is more versatile if you hunt other game such as pheasants, geese or grouse. A 28 inch barrel should not create too much issues as you walk to your hunting spot.

Now let's take a look at what type of shotgun shells you should use with your shotgun...

Step 3: Shotgun Shells and Other Items to Bring Hunting

What Type of Shells Should You Buy?

For effective duck-dropping power, it is important to select the right shotgun shell. Sometimes it can be overwhelming when you walk into a hunting store and see all of the different types of shotgun shells available. In this section I will help you understand some of the differences so you can make a good shell selection the next time you are shopping for shells. Finally, I will also discuss what other items you want to bring hunting with you.

What to consider:

- Shot size
- Shell length
- Price

Shot Size

With shotgun shells one of the choices you will have is the shot size. Basically, the shot size determines how many BBs the shell contains.

Shot sizes (smallest to largest pellet size):

- 6 shot (Smallest BBs)
- 4 shot
- 2 shot
- BB
- BBB
- T (Largest BBs)

Keep in mind, the larger the shot size you choose, the fewer the pellets than can fit in a shell. For example, a 6-shot shell will have more BBs inside than the T-shot. The advantage of more BBs is you get a larger kill radius because there are more BBs in the air to hit your target. The downside is that they have less killing power than larger pellets. The larger the type of duck you are hunting, the larger the shot you will want.

You can also adjust your shot size based on the distance of your shots. The further away your target is, the more power you will need to make the kill. If you get ducks to come in very close range you can use a 4 or sometimes even a 6-shot. However, if you are pass shooting at high-flying ducks then a 2-shot or even a BB-shot is necessary. In general, my recommendation is 2 or 4-shot for most duck hunting situations. If you end up in an area where you notice that you are shooting larger ducks all of the time (like mallards) then going down to a BB-shot can work as well.

Shell Length

Typical shotgun shells range in length from 2 ½ inches to 3 ½ inches. The larger the shell size typically the more range and kill power. However, the longer the shell the more kick it will have when fired. As I mentioned earlier, you need to ensure that you buy the correct size shell length to fit your chamber size. Keep in mind that a larger chambered gun can fit smaller shells. For example, if you buy a gun that has a 3 ½ inch chamber you can actually put 3 inch, 2 ¾ or 2 ½ inch shells in it. In contrast, if you buy a gun with a 3 inch chamber you cannot put 3 ½ inch shells in it.

Shell length options:

- 2 ½ inch
- 2 ¾ inch
- 3 inch
- 3 ½ inch

2 ¾-inch and 3-inch are the most common shell lengths for hunting ducks. Both of these are effective and I use 3-inch in most situations. Some people use 3 ½- inch shells for hunting ducks but in many cases it is not necessary. Using these larger shells can leave you going home with a sore shoulder due to the higher recoil. Additionally, there is a cost difference as you go up in shell length. You can expect to pay about $5 more per box for 3 ½-inch shells than for 3-inch shells. Most importantly you have to remember what the chamber size is on your gun so you know the maximum shell length you can use.

Other Items to Bring Hunting

In addition to your gun, shells, any loose apparel (such as hats, gloves or boots that you might not wear out the door), a duck call (optional – discussed in "Step 18 Duck Calling") and decoys (discussed in Steps 5 and 16), there are a few other items that you should always be sure to have with you when you are going duck hunting.

Flashlight

If you are going hunting early in the morning or plan to be there into the evening hours, you may be traveling to or setting up your hunting site in the dark. So it is best to always have a working flashlight on you. I find it convenient to buy a hat mounted flashlight. Basically it is a light that straps to the front of your hat allowing your hands to be freed up. This is nice when walking to your hunting spot or when you are setting up your decoys.

Compass

A compass is always a nice thing to have on any hunting trip. If you have a phone with a compass, that is a nice option so you don't have an additional item to carry. The compass can not only help you find your way to and from your site, but it can also help you know what direction you are facing as you want to face away from the direction the wind is blowing when hunting ducks. If you look up the wind direction on your phone you may then need to know which way you are facing so you can position yourself accordingly. More on all of this in "Step 13 Wind Direction."

Hunting Knife and other Supplies for Duck Cleaning

If you plan to clean your ducks on site (assuming it is legal in your area – check regulations) you will want to make sure you bring a sharp hunting knife with you. Make sure it is sharp as a dull knife is actually more dangerous being that it will cause you to use more pressure and possibly slip and cut yourself.

You will also want to bring some Ziploc bags for meat or regular plastic grocery bags if you are using the whole duck method. If you want to use gloves when cleaning the duck, remember to bring these as well. It can also be a good idea to bring a cooler with ice regardless of whether you will be cleaning your ducks on site or not. Unless it is cold out or you live very close to home and will be going home within a half hour of shooting, you should have a cooler and ice with you. You will place the whole, uncleaned duck in the cooler if you are not doing the cleaning on site. Make sure the cooler is big enough to hold 3-6 ducks or whatever the legal limit is in your area. See "Step 21 Duck Cleaning" for more information on this process.

Food and Water
Depending on the length of your hunting trip you may want to bring enough food and water so you don't want to have to leave your site in the middle of hunting to get something to eat and you want to make sure you stay hydrated and energized while you are out there. Water is also important to have if you are going to be cleaning your ducks on site and using the whole duck method as you will need to rinse them thoroughly.

Now let's look at licensing and hunter safety...

Step 4: Licensing, Hunter Safety and Rules

Get Your Migratory Game Bird & Applicable Safety Registration

It is important to purchase a hunting license and learn hunting safety prior to heading out for a duck hunting adventure. The laws and regulations for hunting are very different from one area to the next. In the majority of cases you will need to purchase some type of hunting license to be able to hunt ducks. For duck hunting you will also need to purchase an additional federal stamp. Additionally, you may also need to have some type of safety certification prior to purchasing a license.

Honestly, when I first started duck hunting I was quite confused on all of the different licenses and stamps that were required. If you are ever in doubt on what you need just ask the representatives at licensing office and they should be able to get you setup with exactly what you need.

Ensure that you have the proper license and safety certification before doing any type of hunting.

Legal aspects to consider before hunting:

- Area you are hunting
- Specific hunting dates
- Safety certification
- Hunting rules

Area

When you are going to purchase your hunting license, the first thing you will need to know is what area you plan to hunt. Most migratory game bird hunting licenses are good for the entire state that you purchase the license in, but if you will be hunting in multiple states then you will probably need multiple licenses. Be aware that if you are not a resident of the state you plan to hunt in, you will typically pay a higher rate for your license. Sometimes it can be as much as double what it costs for a resident of that state to buy a license.

You should also consider what other type of hunting or fishing you plan to do within that year before you buy a hunting license. Some states allow you to purchase a combination license that will give you hunting and fishing privileges for a discounted rate. Not only do you save money this way, it also helps reduce the amount of paperwork you need to carry with you. Remember that with duck hunting you also need to purchase an additional federal migratory stamp.

Hunting Dates

Not only do you need to know what areas you plan to hunt ducks, you will also need to know the dates you plan to hunt them. Most states' migratory game bird hunting licenses are good for a season. Just be sure you understand the regulations to ensure that you are covered during the dates that you plan to hunt. Unfortunately, not knowing the rules is not a valid excuse if a game warden catches you without proper licensing. The penalties can be very harsh for people who violate the rules including loss of hunting privileges and confiscation of hunting equipment.

Safety Certification

In addition to having proper licensing, you will also need to ensure that you obtain any necessary safety certifications prior to hunting ducks. Again, the rules in each area are different. In some areas you will need to have a formal safety certification regardless of your age. In other areas if you are over a certain age you do not need to have safety training.

Even if your area does not require any safety training, it is an excellent idea to go through a safety training course prior to doing any type of hunting. Although hunting can be a very fun activity, it also comes with a certain level of safety risk. You can never eliminate all safety risks when hunting, but going through a formal safety class will teach you the skills to improve your safety practices. Hunting safety courses often range from $20-$100 for a course that will last a few weeks. This is a great investment in your long-term safety.

Rules

There are also a lot of rules to consider when you go hunting for ducks or any other waterfowl. There are daily limits on how many ducks you can kill and have in your possession so make sure you know these rules before going out. There also might be rules concerning what you need to leave on the duck to take it home. Sometimes you need to leave the whole bird intact for identification in case you are stopped and sometimes just a wing or other body part. So keep this in mind before you start to clean your duck(s).

Now let's take a look at the different types of decoys available for hunting ducks...

Step 5: Decoy Types

What Types of Decoys Are Available?

Using decoys is one of the most popular ways to attract ducks when duck hunting. You lay several of these out in what is called a "spread" to make it look like a realistic situation of several ducks feeding or resting together, usually in a field or in or near water. Here I will discuss the various types of decoys and later in the book I will give examples of effective spreads to use.

There are a wide range of duck decoy types to choose from. The most common decoy that people associate with duck hunting is the floating decoy which is used for hunting ducks over water. However, there are several decoy types to choose from. I will discuss them all here as well as the types of bags available for transporting your decoys.

You will also want to note that within each type of decoy there will be a variety of positions available for purchase such as sitting, feeding, etc. You want to have a variety of positions in your collection to ensure that your setup looks realistic. Some varieties have detachable or swiveling heads to help you to accomplish this variance in positioning.

In addition to there being a variety of positions available within each decoy type, there are also a variety of species. Mallards are a great decoy to use because they are pretty common in most parts of the United States. The other great thing about mallard decoys is that many other ducks will land with mallards making them a very universal decoy to use.

Types of Decoys:

- Full Body Floating Decoys
- Full Body Field Decoys
- Shell Decoys
- Silhouette Decoys
- Windsock Decoys
- Spinning Wing Decoys
- Confidence Decoys

Full Body Floating Decoys

Full body decoys are some of the most realistic duck decoys as they mimic the size, shape, coloring and movement of real ducks. Full body floating decoys are life-size replicas of real ducks. Typically they are made of plastic, foam or wood.

Duck hunting is often done over water, so floating decoys will be an essential part of your hunting gear. The great thing about floating decoys is that they are usually reasonably priced. You can get packs of 6-8 starting around $30.

Floating decoys provide great motion for duck hunting. They have a weight and line attached to the bottom of each decoy that keeps them from floating away while the line allows the decoys to move back and forth with the natural movement of the water and wind. These can also be used in the field with a little adjustment. They can be set directly on the ground as long as you use a little dirt, mud or crops to hold them in place.

The downside to this type of decoy is that they do not stack so they can take up a lot of storage and transport space. You can purchase a mesh bag that allows you to carry several dozen or more together, but be aware that carrying them this way may cause the paint to wear off. (More about this bag later.)

Pros:
- Float in the water and provide life-like motion as the water moves
- Durable
- With a little adjustment they can also be used in the field

Cons:
- Not easy to transport or store as they can't be stacked
- Paint can wear off in transport if you're not careful

Full Body Field Decoys

Similar to full body floating decoys, full body field decoys are realistic and are a great decoy option when you are hunting from a field. Again, these decoys are the same size as a duck and provide excellent visibility due to their size and shape.

You will find that for field hunting these decoys are one of the most effective ways to attract ducks. Many full body duck decoys are on stands called motion stands. These stands allow the decoys to move back and forth in the wind and create a lifelike movement that ducks are attracted to. Other times there are molded legs which can be attached.

However, full body field decoys do have a few downsides which include their high cost and the room required for transport and storage. These decoys are typically the highest cost duck decoys and you can expect to pay $15 or more per decoy. To make transporting a little easier and to protect the decoys, there are slotted bags available that can hold about 6-12 decoys per bag. (More about these bags later.) However, the stands, although normally detachable, are often not collapsible so these take up additional room for storage and transport.

Pros:
- Realistic

- Can add movement with motion stands
- Without motion stands they can appear as sitting or resting
- Highly visible to approaching ducks
- Can be used in a field or on the shore of a body of water

Cons:
- Cost
- Not easy to transport or store as they can't be stacked
- If using stands, these are not collapsible so require additional storage/transport space

Shell Decoys

Shell decoys are life-size (or larger) shell molds of ducks. These also come in "oversized" so they can be used when greater visibility is necessary. They have a hollow interior. These cannot be used in water as they do not float. These decoys can be set on the ground directly or used with motion stakes to elevate them off the ground.

The motion stakes often have a spring-like mechanism on the top allowing the decoys to move up and down as well as back and forth in the wind. Another kind of motion stake simply allows the decoy to move left and right in the wind. In either case they are quite effective and add a level of realism to grab passing ducks.

The pros of shell decoys include their lifelike appearance, their ease of transport, and their ability to add movement to your decoy spread. One of the greatest benefits of shell decoys is how easy they are to stack and store. They fit inside one another allowing you to store and transport a large number of decoys in a small space. The stakes are also easier to store and transport than the stands that come with the full body decoys.

Shell decoys range from $10-$20 per decoy so they are somewhat expensive. Additionally, without proper care they can be damaged or broken. This is because they are made of plastic and are hollow so if you happen to step on or drop one it is possible that you could crack the decoy.

Pros:
- Realistic
- These come in "oversized" as well for greater visibility
- Easy to transport and store; stakes are also easy to transport and store
- With motion stakes add movement to your spread
- Without stakes can appear as sitting or resting
- Can use in the field or on the shore of a body of water

Cons:
- Cost
- Durability
- Difficult to find

Silhouette Decoys

Silhouette decoys are a two-dimensional outline in the shape of a duck. They are typically made of heavy duty cardboard or corrugated plastic but can also be made out of wood or metal. Silhouette decoys are typically very cost effective ranging from $4-$8 per decoy, but you can even make them at home from cardboard to save more money. If you are motivated and are willing to invest the time, this could be a great way to save some money on your hunting accessories. These decoys are great fillers for existing field spreads due to their low cost and ease of transport.

Another benefit of silhouette decoys is that they work well when it is snowing. With full body or shell decoys, snow will collect on the backs of these decoys during a snow storm. Because this is not realistic (as real ducks would not have snow collecting on their backs) and the decoys essentially become hidden from view when this happens, they will become less effective. In contrast, the slim design of silhouette decoys keeps snow from collecting on them, making them a great option for late season field hunting.

Depending on the material they are made of, without proper care, silhouette decoys can be damaged. This is because they can bend or break if you step on them or are not careful when transporting them. The store-bought silhouette decoys are commonly made out of corrugated plastic which is typically quite durable; however, if you make these at home out of cardboard, the decoys will need to be cared for with much more attention to ensure they are not damaged. Also if they are cardboard they would not hold up as well in the rain.

The other consideration with silhouette decoys is that you need to have a significant amount of them to be effective. This is because they are two-dimensional so if you face them all in one direction the ducks will be unable to see them when approaching your decoy spread from the side. You need to have at least a few dozen of these faced all different directions so that regardless of the angle the birds are approaching from, they can still see several decoys.

Pros:
- Low cost
- Easy to transport and store; stake is also easy to store and transport
- Great filler with other decoys
- Work well in the snow
- Can use in the field or on the shore of a body of water

Cons:
- Can be fragile, depending on material
- If made of cardboard these might not do so well in the rain
- Need many of these to be effective

Windsock Decoys

Windsock decoys are not as common as the other decoy types but they can be effective when hunting from fields. Windsock decoys have a body made out of a fabric or plastic connected to a stake. They usually require wind to fill them up and make them look like the body of a duck. Some have a backbone which holds up the decoy body and allows them to look realistic without the wind. Some also have a more realistic firmer plastic duck head on them.

The low cost of windsock decoys makes them an attractive option as they are usually less than $5 per decoy. You can carry a significant amount of these decoys in a storage tote or decoy bag. Additionally, they can create great movement for your spread because they are designed to catch the wind and produce motion. Wind collects in the body and since it is on a stake in the ground this allows it to float freely back and forth as the wind blows. This creates an appearance of ducks walking in the field.

These decoys need to be properly cared for. They can get dirty if they touch the ground, and being dirty will make them look unnatural to approaching ducks. As you set them up and take them down, be sure to keep them off the ground so they stay as clean as possible. Also, if you get decoys without heads, or if you do not have much wind they may not look as real as other decoy types. To be most effective they need wind, so if you are hunting a calm day they might not be the best option unless you have the type with a backbone.

Pros:
- Low cost
- Easy to transport
- Create motion
- Can use in the field or on the shore of a body of water

Cons:
- Fragile if not properly cared for
- Can get dirty
- Without head they might not look as realistic as other decoys
- Typically need wind to be effective (unless you have the type with a backbone)

Spinning Wing Decoys

Spinning wing decoys are duck decoys that have wings that spin around in circles creating a flying and landing appearance and can be a very effective way to attract ducks. These decoys are typically put on a 4-6 foot pole to keep them above the water or field. The height of the decoy on the pole increases its visibility to ducks. The flapping motion on these decoys is created by battery, wind or even by pulling a string. Some of the battery-powered spinning wing decoys are remote-operated. This is a convenient feature as you can save battery power while you set up your decoys or during a lull in the hunting. You can quickly turn the decoys on when you see ducks approaching.

Spinning wing decoys can be effective in catching the eyes of passing ducks. They mimic the look of a real duck flying and/or landing so ducks will feel comfortable coming to your spread. These decoys are most effective when used in conjunction with other decoys. Typically you would only use 1-3 of these in addition to your existing decoy spread. If you had an entire decoy spread made of just these decoys it would look unnatural to approaching ducks and would likely be ineffective. It is most effective to put these facing into the front third of the densest part of your spread and make it look as though the ducks are heading to land there.

Durability can be an issue for these decoys if they are not properly cared for, as moving parts on any device always make them more fragile and require extra maintenance. The good news is that most of these decoys come with some sort of carrying case which provides protection.

In addition, you do need to check the regulations for your area before using spinning wing decoys. Some areas do not allow spinning wing decoys at all and some areas only allow non-motorized versions of these decoys. This is particularly true on state and federal hunting lands where the regulations tend to be stricter than on private property.

Pros:
- Provides great movement
- Eye catching
- Realistic

Cons:
- Can be fragile and require maintenance
- Not legal in all areas
- Cost

Confidence Decoys

This is not so much a type of decoy as it is a variety. Confidence decoys are decoys of other birds that are commonly seen with ducks so it can be of any of the types previously discussed. The purpose of using these is to make your decoy setup look natural to approaching ducks as ducks often congregate with other birds in real life. The most common confidence decoys that are used with duck decoys are goose decoys. However, there are other types you can use as well.

Confidence decoy types:
- Geese
- Swans
- Seagulls
- Sand Hill Cranes
- Coots

Pay attention to what kinds of birds hang out with the ducks in your area. If you see that ducks in your area hang out with a particular type of bird most often, then it would be a good idea to get a few of those decoys to add to your spread. All you need to do is add a few groups of these birds at the edges of your spread and you are all set. Even 1-2 of these mixed in your spread can work wonders in pulling in more ducks. You also have the possibility of pulling in other birds when you use these.

Another benefit of confidence decoys is to help make your decoy spread stand out from other hunters' in the area, particularly if you are hunting in an area where there is a lot of competition. The ducks will actually get used to seeing decoys in highly hunted areas so if you can do something to change up your spread and make it look more realistic than the next hunter's, you can be at a great advantage.

Decoy Bags

Now that you have learned about all of the different types of decoys, let's look at some ways you can transport them. The good news is there are a wide range of decoy bags available on the market to transport and store nearly every type of decoy.

Slotted Bags (for Full Body Field Decoys)

For full body field decoys the bags are often referred to as "slotted" bags meaning they have a certain amount of slots to hold decoys. Typically "slotted" bags have room for 6-12 decoys. The "slotted" bags will be the most expensive bag, but if you have invested in the high cost of full body field decoys than it is probably a good idea to invest in bags that will help protect your decoys.

Mesh Bags (for Floating Duck Decoys)

For floating duck decoys it is best to use a mesh decoy bag which can be carried on your back similar to a backpack. This makes it very convenient to carry many decoys to your favorite hunting spot. With the mesh design you do not have to worry about water getting trapped inside of your bag. You can toss your full decoy bag in the water as you set up and when you have all of your decoys out you can simply ball up the bag for easy storage while you hunt.

Satchel Bag (for Silhouette or Windsock Decoys)

If you elect to go with silhouette or windsock decoys there are satchel bags available. Basically you stack all of your silhouette or windsock decoys together and then you place them into a flat carrying bag which goes nicely over your shoulder. I own one of these bags and can easily transport and store several dozen decoys in a single bag.

So What Decoys Should You Buy?

The answer to this question is really determined by your specific situation. Before you invest in decoys I suggest that you ask yourself these questions to help you with your decoy selection.

- Will you be hunting water or fields?
- How much storage room do you have?
- What is your vehicle capable of transporting?
- How much can you afford?

Now let's see how to find the ducks…

Step 6: How to Find the Ducks

It Can Take Some Research to Find the Ducks

Let's take a look at some good ways to figure out where the ducks are. This is a critical step in having duck hunting success. In fact, this is probably one of the largest determinants of being able to bag ducks because regardless of how well you do all of the other elements of duck hunting, if there are no ducks in the area you will not shoot any.

How to know where to find ducks:

- Pay attention to where ducks are flying
- Check rivers and streams
- Check local fields
- Check ponds/holding areas
- Open water in the winter
- Use your network of friends and family

Pay Attention to Where Ducks Are Flying

This should be obvious but you want to pay attention to where you see ducks. When you are driving around keep an eye out in the air to see where ducks are flying. Maybe you notice that ducks are always flying in a certain direction on your way to work each day. This might be a great opportunity to take a Saturday morning and follow the ducks using your same route to work. You just might follow the ducks to a hidden gem of a hunting spot.

Check Rivers and Streams

Like most waterfowl, ducks like easy-to-find water sources and places to rest during the day. Rivers and streams are some of the best places to find ducks. Hunting on rivers can be an exciting way to hunt ducks because they will often come from up or down river and seemingly appear out of nowhere. When this happens you can get some very exciting shooting in.

When you are looking for ducks on rivers and streams you should be sure to check the edges. Ducks are easy to see when they are sitting out in the middle of a river but that is not always where they rest. Ducks will often rest very near the riverbank and some hunters overlook checking these spots. It can be difficult to see ducks in this location but if you pay attention you might discover ducks that other hunters have overlooked.

The one downside of hunting rivers and streams is retrieving your ducks. If you shoot ducks on a river you will most likely either need a dog or boat to get them out of the water. You could try going in yourself with waders, but depending on how deep the water gets it might not be possible.

Check Local Fields

Fields are another place that ducks will go for a source of food and rest. Some of their favorite types of fields are corn, alfalfa and hay. If you run across a field that has a low spot with some standing water then you have truly run across what should be a gold mine for hunting ducks. (More about hunting fields in "Step 7 Hunting Crop Fields.")

Check Ponds & Holding Areas

Anytime you can find a sizeable spot of standing water there is a chance that you will find ducks there. Some farmers have watering trenches that are used to water their crops. These holding ponds are prime spots for ducks as they not only have access to water but quick access to the field of crops as well. Sometimes you can find small ponds in woods which ducks use as landing spots. A particular species of duck that likes these ponds are wood ducks. They like to be near the woods and have a tendency to land in some smaller bodies of water.

Open Water In The Winter

In addition to the fact that ducks like rivers, lakes and ponds, these areas can be highly effective during the winter in the open water spots. What I mean is that if you live in an area where the water freezes over during the winter months than any areas where the water remains unfrozen can be great hunting spots. Sometimes just one section of a lake is unfrozen and if you can setup your decoys there the ducks will love it. They need somewhere to rest and drink so if you are in the only open water spot around you should be in for some good hunting.

Use Your Network of Friends and Family

It can be advantageous to ask your friends and family to be on the lookout for ducks for you. Let them know that you want to go duck hunting and ask if they can pay attention to where they are seeing ducks. It is better to have several people searching for ducks rather than just you, and often friends and family will be willing to help you out with this.

One quick way you can solicit the help of friends and family is by making a post to your favorite social media website. This is a great way to get the word out to a lot of people at once. Keep in mind that if any of these hunting spots are on private property you will have to get permission from the owner to hunt there.

Now let's discuss the types of crop fields that are good to hunt...

Step 7: Hunting Crop Fields

Types of Crop Fields that Are Good for Hunting Duck

Here I will look at the types of crop fields that are good for duck hunting and some advantages to and strategies for hunting each. Other than alfalfa fields where the crop is very low, you will have to wait until crops are harvested in most fields before hunting them, but if you can find a partially-harvested field or one with an open spot next to standing crop, this can work well. If you can find standing water in a crop field that is even more ideal.

We will discuss later in the book how in a partially-harvested field (or one with an open spot next to standing crop) the remaining crops can be used for concealment. In that situation you would follow the advice below on what decoys to use based on the state of the harvested portion of the field. You will always want to leave about 15-20 yards between any crops and a decoy spread because ducks will not land next to crops for fear of predators lurking within.

Field types:

- Chopped Corn Fields
- Clear Cut Corn Fields
- Alfalfa Fields (before or after harvest)
- Hay Fields (after harvest)

Chopped Corn Fields

A chopped corn field means a field that has been harvested and a fairly large portion of the corn stalk has been left at the bottom, sometimes as much as 2 feet. The benefit to this is that these left-behind stalks can be used as excellent cover for hiding (more about concealing yourself for hunting later in the book). This is in contrast to clear cut corn fields leaving behind no stalks or just a few inches of the corn stalk and hardly anything to use as cover.

However, the problem with chopped corn fields is they can create some visibility issues for ducks to see your decoys if you are using them. As long as you use elevating stakes or stands on your decoys though you should be okay. All the types of decoys mentioned in

"Step 5 Decoy Types" can be used in this type of location as long as they can be put up high enough so the ducks can see over any remaining corn stalks.

Clear Cut Corn Fields

The advantage of hunting clear cut corn fields is that the short stocks left behind will allow the ducks to see pretty much every type of decoy you put out. Essentially, a clear cut corn field is a corn field that has been cut down and there is really not much of the corn stalks left behind. Typically these fields might have the very bottom few inches of the corn stalks left and the rest of the field is dirt. A downside of these fields is that they can present a challenge in concealing yourself as there is not much natural covering left behind to use. Any type of decoy could work in this location type even if you don't have elevating stakes or stands as any remaining crop should be very low to the ground and not hindering visibility.

Alfalfa Fields

Another field type that can provide good success for hunting ducks is alfalfa fields. These fields present plenty of nutrients for ducks and can attract Canada geese and other waterfowl as well. The height of the alfalfa will determine what decoys you should use. When it is still growing it can be 6-12 inches tall, but when it is harvested, the remaining crop is usually 2-3 inches high. This crop does not tend to provide as much in the way of cover for concealing the hunter as a corn or hay field. Make sure that any decoys you use are placed high enough to be seen over the crops.

Hay Fields

A great benefit of hay fields is that they will typically provide plenty of cover to conceal the hunter. The long, tall grass-like reeds in these fields are ideal for cover and there is often enough left behind on the ground after harvest to use for this purpose. When the hay is cut and rolled or when it is cut and laid out to dry you can take advantage of these situations as spots to sit decoys. Any decoys should work in a harvested hay field as there are no visibility issues.

Now let's take a look at how to get permission to hunt private property…

Step 8: How to Get Permission to Hunt Private Land

Tips for Asking Permission

If you are like me, you do not own hunting land and don't always want to battle other hunters for public land. In addition, crop fields which are typically private property, provide some of the best locations for duck hunting. At first it can feel a little uncomfortable to ask other people to use their land for hunting; however, after some experience the process gets much easier. Also, if you get permission to hunt on someone's land one time, they are likely to let you come back again in the future.

Tips to get permission to hunt private land:

- Don't be afraid to ask
- Don't wear hunting clothes when approaching them to ask
- Be kind and smile
- Bring a youth hunter if possible
- Tell them exact times you will be there
- Do a favor in return
- Bring them meat or another gift
- Thank them after

Don't Be Afraid to Ask

Something that holds hunters back from finding land to hunt is the fear of asking for permission. People can feel intimidated by asking landowners for permission to hunt on their property. I shared the same fear when I first started hunting, but the more you do it the more you get used to it. When you are turned down, the primary reason is that they already have a friend or family member that hunts the area. I have never had anyone get upset at me for asking.

Sample wording to use when asking permission:

- Hello, my name is ___ and I am hoping to do some duck hunting tomorrow. It seems like you have a great piece of land for duck hunting. Would it be okay with you if I hunted on your property this weekend?

- Good afternoon, I am looking for a place to duck hunt with my daughter tomorrow. Would it be possible for us to hunt on your land for ducks for a few hours in the afternoon?

- Hello, I was driving by and I saw several ducks in your fields. I really enjoy duck hunting and I'm wondering if it would be okay with you if I could hunt here for a few hours today.

If they say "no," don't waste this opportunity to find a hunting spot. Say "Thank you, I understand. Do you happen to know of any other places nearby that you would suggest that I try?" They might know another landowner that would allow you to hunt nearby or they might know of some good public land for hunting in the area.

Don't Wear Hunting Clothing

I recommend not wearing hunting clothing when you go to ask for permission to hunt on someone's property because it can give the landowners a feeling that you are assuming that you will be able to hunt there. Not all people like or allow hunting so don't assume anything.

If you are planning on hunting that same day, at least take off your camouflage clothing. It should not take too much to remove the items that make you look like a hunter. If you are dressed like you are ready to hunt, it can also give them the impression that you may trespass on their land even if they do not give you permission.

Be Kind and Smile

This should go without saying but if you are polite to the landowner they will more than likely be polite back. Be conscious when you approach the property to put a smile on your face to ensure that you are received as a friendly individual.

Be sure to make the impression that you are friendly and easy to get along with. Do what you can to strike up a conversation with the landowner by asking them some questions such as how long they have lived at the property and what they do for a living. People love to talk about themselves so if you can get the conversation going and let the landowner talk, it will likely improve your chances of getting permission to hunt their land.

If they do agree to allow you to hunt on their property, keep the conversation going and ask them where on their property in particular they would recommend hunting. After all, they should know best where the ducks have been on their property.

Bring a Youth Hunter

Most people have a soft spot for children and if you are planning on hunting with a child it can help to bring them with you when you ask for permission. People who would have said no to you alone may say yes if it means that a child will get the opportunity to experience the outdoors. Another benefit of bringing a child is that it can be a great learning experience for them. This helps get the child used to speaking to strangers and helps them learn all of the aspects of hunting that will be valuable to them when they start hunting on their own.

Tell Them the Exact Times You Will Be There

To help put the landowners at ease, it is important to let them know exactly when you plan to hunt. If you want to hunt just one morning, tell them that. Or if you want access for an entire weekend, be specific so they are not taken off guard when they see you on their property. This is very important because people will feel more comfortable knowing the exact times that they can expect to see you rather than having you show up at any random time of the day. Never go hunting on someone else's property at a time when you do not have permission.

Do a Favor In Return

Landowners often have work that needs to be done around their property, particularly if they are farmers. Ask them if there are a few projects that you could help out with for an afternoon or two in exchange for hunting on their property. Not only would assisting with these chores be a way to get permission to hunt, it is also a great way to form a relationship with the landowner. The more you get to know them, the more likely they are to let you to continue to hunt there.

Bring them Meat or Other Small Gifts

Another thing you can ask is if the landowners would like to have some meat in exchange for allowing you to hunt there. Even if they don't hunt, most people may like getting some free meat. This can be a great win-win situation for both parties. Not all people like duck meat so you could bring some other type of small gift as a way to say thank you to the landowner for allowing you to use their property. You could bake some cookies in advance or stop at the store on the way and buy some cookies to give them. It does not have to be anything very expensive but something simple can go a long way in letting them know that you appreciate their generosity in allowing you to hunt on their property.

Benefits of Getting Permission Effectively

If you follow these steps and are respectful with those who allow you to hunt their land, you may end up with one or more long-term hunting spots. Be kind when asking, do something in return, and get to know the landowners. The better the connections you make with people, the more likely you will be to build a great network of landowners and have multiple hunting locations that you can use.

The next step covers finding public land for duck hunting...

Step 9: Finding Public Land to Hunt

Public Land Can Provide Excellent Hunting Opportunities

Similar to private land, with a little effort you can find some great hunting spots available on public land. The downside to using public land is you will have competition for space.

Types of public land available for hunting:

- Wildlife Management Areas (WMAs)
- Waterfowl Production Areas (WPAs)
- State Forests
- Wildlife Refuges
- National Forests

- County Land

Tips about using public land:

- Search online
- Contact your state wildlife office
- Scout out the area in advance
- Be safe

Search Online

With a little online research you will be sure to find some public hunting land within a reasonable driving distance from your home. Simply search online using any of the terms listed above under "Types of public land available for hunting" followed by your state or county name and there will be a listing. Each state has different regulations for these areas so if you have questions regarding hunting regulations that are not clearly denoted online, be sure to reach out to your state wildlife office directly.

Contact Your State Wildlife Office

State wildlife officers are usually very friendly people and passionate about the outdoors. Don't be afraid to call the wildlife office and ask them what areas they would suggest nearby for duck hunting. They want to help people enjoy the outdoors so if you ask, they are going to be happy to assist.

Scout Out the Area in Advance

Once you have a site in mind, if possible, it is great to scout out the area in advance. Try driving to the hunting location a few days prior to actually hunting and review the territory. Take a walk and note where you see ducks.

Even if you are unable to physically go to the hunting spot in advance, you can use online resources to help you plan your hunt. Since you may have found this location by looking online for public hunting areas, you can usually find online maps for these public lands as well. Scan those maps to determine where you will hunt and the route you will take to your hunting spot in advance.

Safety

Safety is the primary thing to be aware of when hunting on public land. Since it is public land, anyone can use this land and there is no way to guarantee that you are alone. It is important to check your surroundings before you shoot. It is easy to get caught up in the excitement of shooting and forget what is around you. You want to think about what is in the direction you are shooting as bullets can travel a long distance. You need to be 100% sure that there is nobody in the vicinity that could possibly get hit. If you are ever in doubt if you have a safe shot, do not shoot.

Now let's look at the duck hunting season…

Step 10: The Duck Hunting Season

Opportunities and Challenges Change During the Season

One thing that keeps hunting ducks exciting throughout the entire season is that you will get new and unique hunting opportunities as the year progresses. Each of the four major flyways in the United Sates has different duck migration patterns but what you can expect is that you will see different species of ducks as the year progresses. The dates of the hunting season will vary from state to state so be sure to check the regulations for your area. Please note that this is a generic summary of the duck season and can vary from region to region.

This section covers the different parts of the season:

- Early Season
- Mid-Season
- Late Season

Early Season

Opening weekend of duck hunting is by far my favorite part of the season. On many opening weekends within an hour I have hit the limit on ducks that I can shoot that day. In many areas early season is the best time for duck hunting success. The ducks have not been hunted for a year so they are not as wary as they are later in the season.

In the early season you will also usually have more access to natural coverings for concealment. The grass on the side of water hunting spots will likely be tall and full. This will provide excellent hiding locations. In addition if you are using decoys you will not need to use as many at this time of year as you would later in the season. Ducks are not yet migrating and therefore there are only smaller, local groups around. In order for your spread to be realistic you would want to keep it small as well.

Another benefit of the early season is that many other hunters are out in the surrounding areas which helps push ducks to fly from one feeding area to the next. This can create some great hunting opportunities throughout the day. The downside of hunting early season is competing with other hunters for land. If you have private land this is not an issue but if you hunt public land than you need to take this into consideration. Make sure you arrive at the hunting spot you picked out very early to ensure it is not taken.

Mid-Season

As the year progresses you will see more and more migrating birds come to your area. The challenge is mid-season birds have now had hunting pressure and will begin to be more difficult to draw into your spread.

The amount of hunters out typically decreases due to the colder weather but you will still have plenty of competition. In order to be successful in the mid-season consider doing something different with your decoy spread than the other hunters as these differences might just be enough to draw in those wary ducks.

Adding confidence decoys at this time can be great. Try adding in a few goose decoys to bring up the ducks' level of comfort. Chances are you might even be able to bag a few geese while you are at it. In general at this time you will want your spreads to include a larger number of decoys than in the early season.

You can also try different calling techniques. One strategy is to completely stop calling and let the ducks come naturally. Try out new things and see what works for you in your specific area. (More about calling in "Step 18 Duck Calling.")

Late Season

The late season can still provide some excellent hunting opportunities. One benefit of hunting late into the season is many hunters have already given up for the year making it easier to find open hunting spots without having to arrive super early.

A key to late season success is finding open water. By this time of year many of the smaller ponds and lakes have frozen over and ducks will be looking for open sources of water. This means that if you have been hunting ponds earlier in the year you will need to find some new hunting spots. Start looking for larger lakes and rivers that are not frozen for the best hunting opportunities. If you are using decoys, you would want to put out the maximum number that you can at this point as the migration has increased the bird population.

Let's see how to have duck hunting success all day long…

Step 11: Time of Day to Hunt

Each Part of the Day Has Benefits for Hunting

Morning, afternoon and evening all have some advantages for duck hunting. Try hunting all different times to see what works best for you and your area. I have had success duck hunting at all times of the day. You just need to prioritize when you are able to hunt and balance that with the likeliness of seeing ducks. Also make sure you know the rules for legal hunting times in your area.

In this section I will discuss the times of day and how each can be effective for duck hunting:

Times of day:

- Morning
- Afternoon
- Sunset (if legal)

Mornings

Taking advantage of the morning feeding time is an excellent way to bag some ducks. As the sun comes up in the morning the ducks begin to get off their resting spots and head out to feed. If you are set up in your duck hunting spot first thing in the morning the chances are that you will get some excellent hunting opportunities.

Personally, I think the morning is one of the best times of the day to go duck hunting as you get to see the outdoors wake up. When you get to a hunting spot before the sun rises you can hear all of the noises that happen as the sun comes up. You can hear a wide range of wildlife wake up and start their day.

Afternoon

It is possible to have duck hunting success later in the day depending on where you are set up. Typically after mid-morning the amount of birds moving about will slow down; however, if you are patient, it is possible to pick up a few ducks in the afternoon. Sometimes by staying put you allow the movement of other hunters heading home to drive more birds your way. These hunters might walk past ducks that are resting and cause them to fly to another location.

Sunset

Some of the most productive hunts I have ever had have been at sunset. Similar to morning hunts, the ducks often come back off their resting spots in order to feed. They will be heading back out for their final meal of the day. Check your local regulations for hunting times in your area. Some hunting zones allow evening hunting in the early season but cut off evening hunting at 4pm during the mid and late season.

Now let's look at the number of decoys you should be using for your spread...

Step 12: Number of Decoys to Use

How Many Decoys Should You Use?

When using decoys, the number of decoys you use in your spread can be an important factor in effectively hunting ducks. Many people think that the more decoys you use the more success you will have with duck hunting, but this is not necessarily always the case. The ideal amount depends on many factors.

Factors impacting the number of decoys in your spread:

- Time of year
- Decoy type
- Number of hunters
- Size of body of water or size of field
- Number of ducks using the area

- Your budget

Time of Year

As discussed in "Step 10 The Duck Hunting Season," in general, you will want to increase the number of decoys in your spread as the hunting season progresses. This is because as the season progresses, the size of the flocks of ducks you will see increases due to the progressing migration.

Early Season

When you are hunting the early season you will typically be hunting local ducks. These flocks are usually smaller since they are local and have not had a chance to congregate with other ducks yet.

Number of Decoys: 3-12

Smaller spreads in the early season can be effective, particularly if you have full body decoys or oversized shell decoys that provide excellent visibility. Since you will see smaller groups of 2-12 birds at this time of year, the smaller spreads are more realistic. Having an extremely large decoy spread this early in the year can actually look unnatural to ducks and they might not be attracted to the spread. Another reason that these small decoy spreads can work in the early season is the fact that the ducks have not had much hunting pressure yet. This means that early season ducks will feel comfortable landing with a smaller flock of ducks.

Mid-Season

As the season progresses the number of ducks migrating to your area will likely increase. This means that if you have more decoys this is a great time to bring them with you to your favorite hunting spot.

Number of Decoys: 12-24

In the mid-season, ducks are beginning to connect with other migrating ducks and it is not uncommon to see flocks of 12-30 ducks. This means that you will probably want to move up to decoy spreads of 12-24 decoys. Additionally, the ducks have now begun to feel hunting pressure and might have been shot at several times at this point. For flocks to feel comfortable landing, they want to see larger flocks on the ground as they have a tendency to feel more comfortable joining up with these larger numbers.

Late Season

The late season calls for the largest decoy spreads. Ducks are now in full migration and the flocks are large.

Number of Decoys: 24-50+

This does not mean that you cannot have success with smaller numbers of decoys, especially if you get solo birds flying by; however, in order to pull in larger flocks, larger spreads are likely going to be needed. In the late season try to mix up how you set up your decoys. By this time of year ducks have been hunted hard for a few months and are used to seeing decoys. Try adjusting your setup to make your spread stand out from any others that might be around and make it look more realistic.

Decoy Type

The types of decoys you are using can significantly impact the numbers you will need in your duck decoy spreads. As I outlined earlier, common decoy types include full body, shell, windsock, and silhouette decoys. For those who hunt with full body floating or field decoys they can sometimes get away with smaller duck spreads because full body duck decoys typically have the greatest visibility out of all of the decoy types. Oversized shell decoys also have great visibility for ducks.

In contrast, hunters using silhouette decoys are going to need a significantly larger number of decoys in their duck decoy spreads. This is because silhouette decoys are two-dimensional and can only be seen when they are facing approaching ducks. For silhouette decoys to be effective, you need to have several dozen of them facing a variety of directions so that regardless of the angle that the ducks are approaching from they will be able to see some of the decoys.

Number of Hunters

If the hunters in your party are hunting from within the spread and using the decoys for concealment you would want to apply a formula to determine the number of decoys to use. A common ratio of decoys to hunters is 2 dozen decoys per hunter in your party. So if you have 6 hunters and use this formula you would need at least 12 dozen (144 decoys) in the spread.

Below is an example of two hunters using the 2 dozen decoy ratio = 48 Decoys

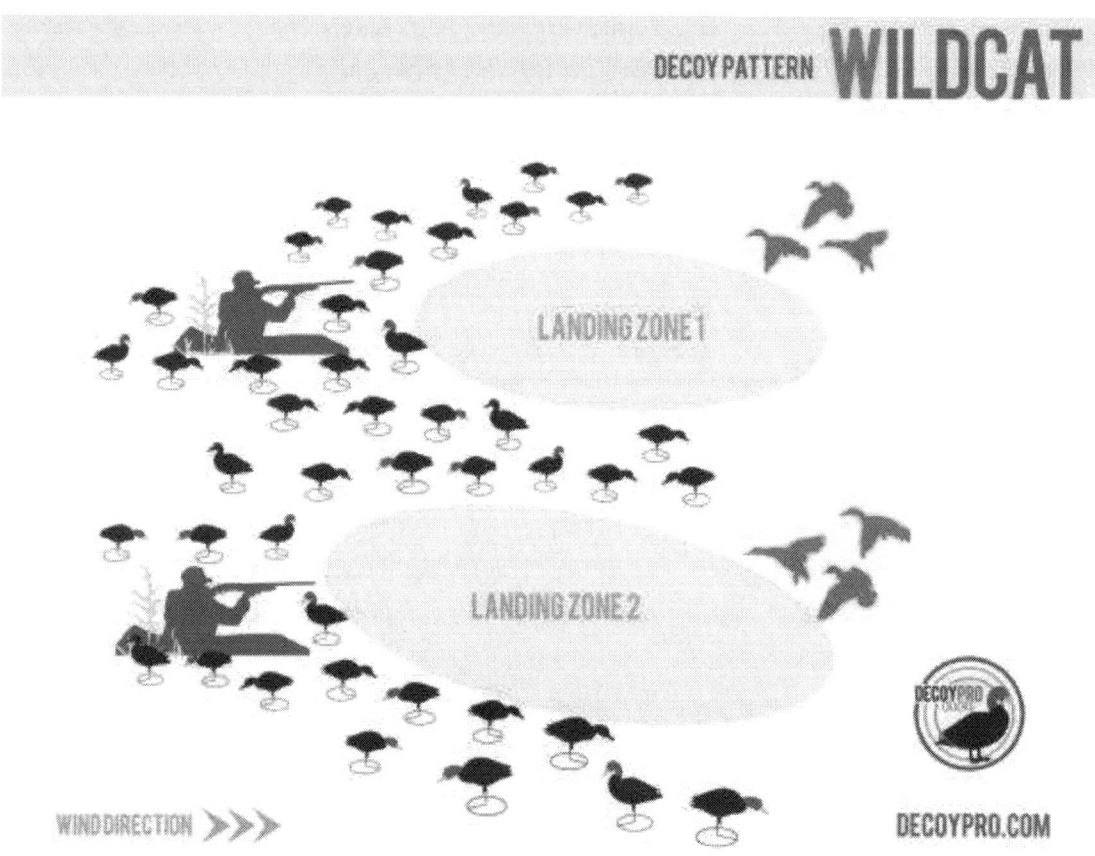

Below is an example of two hunters using a 1 dozen decoy ratio = 24 Decoys

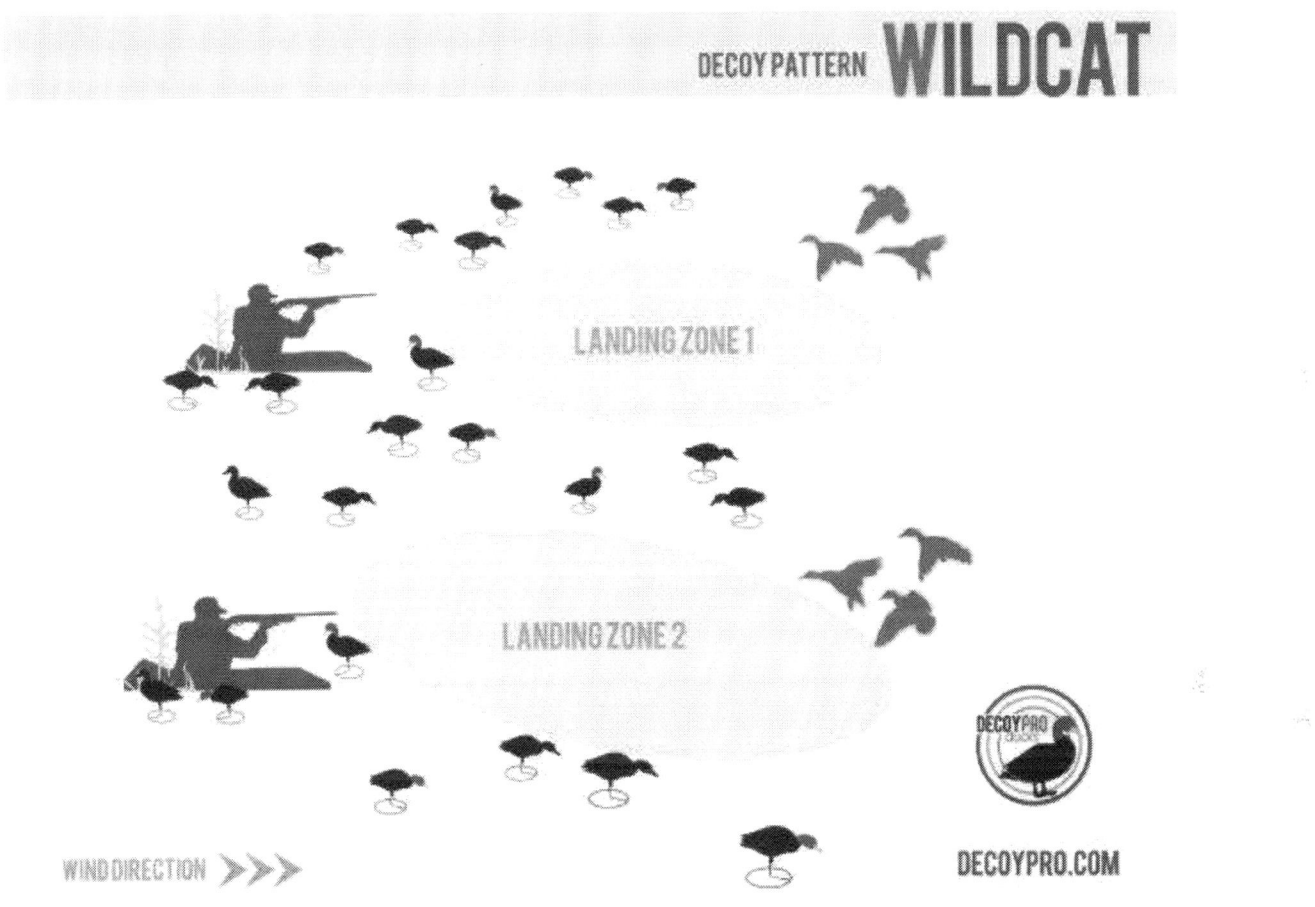

From the above examples you can clearly see how using 2 dozen decoys (first example) instead of 1 dozen decoys (second example) per hunter would be much more effective in concealing the hunters. Of course if you do not have that many decoys you will just need to use what you have until you can expand your spread; however, this is a good ratio to strive for when you are able to invest in more decoys

Size of Body of Water

In general, the larger the body of water you are hunting, the larger the spread you should use. You will notice this when you pay attention to ducks in your area. It is likely for a lot of ducks to be resting on large bodies of water. However, you are probably not going to see hundreds of ducks sitting on a small pond.

Lakes, Wide Rivers, and Oceans

Hunting a large lake, a wide river, or even an ocean could call for several dozen decoys to grab the attention of ducks. This is because the ducks have a large area to look at as they fly over and a small spread would be lost. In addition, even with the greater number of decoys, the large area of water will still allow for a sufficient landing zone.

Ponds and Narrow Rivers

A small pond or narrow river calls for a much smaller spread size. For example, I often hunt over a pond that is only about 60 yards long and 30 yards wide. Since the pond is so small I typically set out 3-6 decoys. This is to ensure that I leave plenty of room for the approaching ducks to land. If I were to put out more decoys it would crowd the ducks and they would likely fly past and never get within shotgun range.

Size of Field

Similar in concept to the size of the body of water you are hunting, the size of a field you hunt also plays a role in your decoy spread size. When you are hunting a large field with not much else around, you need more decoys to grab the attention of passing ducks. However, when you hunt a field that is small you would want to use many fewer.

Number of Ducks Using the Area

If you are lucky enough to be hunting in the exact area that ducks are landing, you can most likely get away with using a smaller number of decoys than if ducks were not landing there at all. For example, let's say you have scouted out a field where you saw hundreds of ducks feeding on the recently cut corn. You could probably put out just a few dozen decoys and have success. And if the ducks frequented there enough, you may not need any decoys at all, or very few.

However, if you are hunting an area where the ducks are not landing regularly, then you probably need more decoys. This is because you need to give those passing-by ducks a reason to come to that spot. Placing several dozen feeding decoys out can draw the interest of the passing-by ducks. When they see a lot of ducks feeding in one area they will likely think there is plenty of food and might be interested in joining in on the feast.

Budget

Of course another thing to factor into your decoy spread size is the amount of money that you have to invest in decoys. If you need to be cautious of how much you spend on decoys, it should help to know that the first decoys I ever bought were purchased on Craigslist and they only cost me $40 for two dozen shell decoys. Simply start off with what you can afford and then when you have some extra cash either add more decoys or upgrade your current spread. Also see "Step 17 Hunting Without Decoys" if you want to try this first before investing in decoys that you may not need.

Final Words on Decoy Spread Size

In general, larger spreads can be very effective for hunting ducks. However, it is important to consider all the factors discussed above before making a determination on how many decoys you need to put in your spread on any given day. Time of year, decoy type, the size of the body of water and/or field you are hunting and the number of hunters in your party will all impact the number of decoys you need in your spread to effectively hunt ducks.

I encourage you to use these recommendations as a starting point for your decoy spread size, but I also want to encourage you to be willing to adjust. If you find that large decoy spreads are not working, try playing around with small spreads and vary the way you set up your spreads. If you use trial and error you will eventually find out what works best for you and your particular hunting situation(s).

Now let's learn how wind direction impacts duck hunting...

Step 13: Wind Direction

Using Wind to Your Advantage

To understand how to set up your decoys and position yourself for hunting, you first need to understand how ducks use wind for landing. The most important thing to know is that ducks like to land into the wind. They like to do this because it allows them to use the natural lift of the wind to have a gentle landing.

To understand this compare it to the way a kite behaves. When you fly a kite and it is facing into the wind it will be held up in the air nicely; however, if the kite gets turned around and is going with the wind the kite speeds up and crashes into the ground. Ducks experience the same thing when landing, so they simply face into the wind to use the natural lift to make a smooth landing onto the ground or water.

Now that you know that ducks want to land into the wind, you can effectively plan the setup of your decoys and your positioning for better hunting success. In the majority of the cases you want to have your back to the wind. This way the approaching ducks will be landing in the direction you are facing allowing you direct shots at them.

Wind direction impacts:

- Decoy setup
- Blind setup
- Hunter positioning

You will see many diagrams later in the book when I reveal different decoy layouts, but right now I am just showing these diagrams to point out that the decoy setup and the hunter's position are both based on the direction of the wind. On all future diagrams you will see that the wind direction is indicated at the bottom of the picture.

Wind Examples
Example 1: Wind Blowing Left to Right (Land & Water).

Duck Hunting Made Simple: 21 Steps to Duck Hunting Success

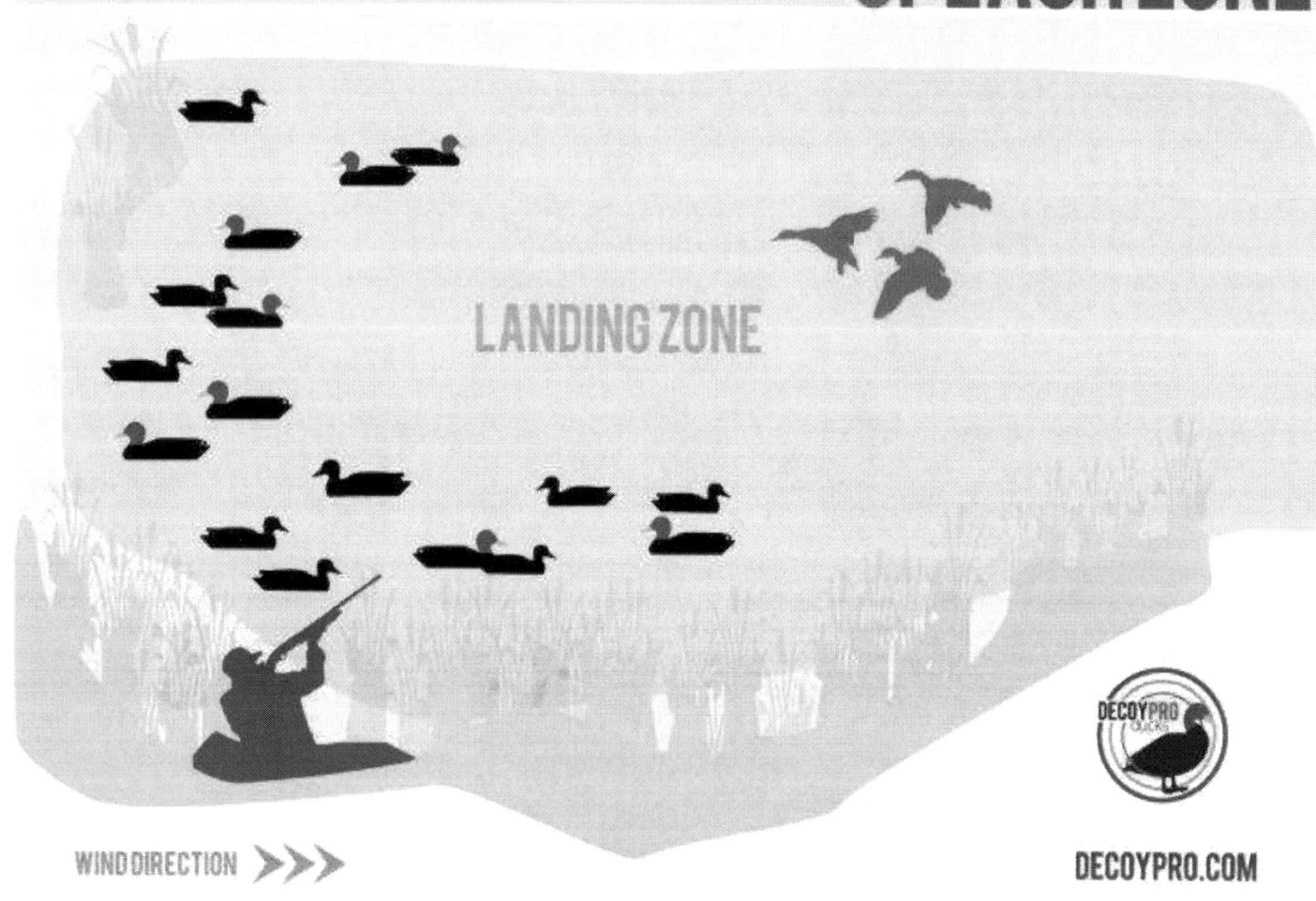

You can see in the above diagrams that the approaching ducks are flying directly into the wind and the positioning of the landing zone is set up to take advantage of this. You will also notice that the hunter is placed with his back to the wind. In many hunting situations, particularly when you are hunting from within your decoys, you will want to be positioned with your back to the wind. At times, as in the second diagram, you will be slightly off to the side of your spread, but your back would pretty much still be to the wind.

Example 2: Wind Blowing Right to Left (Land & Water)

Duck Hunting Made Simple: 21 Steps to Duck Hunting Success

You can see in these examples the wind is now blowing from right to left and the approaching ducks are again flying directly into the wind. The change of wind direction from the first two diagrams to the second two diagrams simply changed the direction of the decoy spread and the hunter. Remember to always have the opening of the decoy spread and the hunter facing the opposite direction of the way that the wind is blowing.

How Do You Know Which Direction the Wind is Blowing?
This may seem like an easy answer but sometimes it can be challenging to determine which way the wind is blowing. Here are a few ways you can do this:

- You can use your phone with a weather app to identify the wind direction, then use the position of the sun or a compass to determine your direction and position yourself accordingly.
- Look at nearby flags to see which way the wind is blowing them.
- Grab a small handful of grass or dirt and hold it chest high. Let it go and look for the direction it goes as it heads towards the ground.

I will discuss later on in the book what to do if the wind changes directions or if there is no wind at all.

Now let's find out how other weather conditions impact duck hunting...

Step 14: Impact of Weather

How Does Weather Impact Duck Hunting?

Besides wind, there are other types of weather that affect duck hunting. The type of weather you are experiencing can greatly impact how and where you set up your decoys, the type of decoys you use and where you hunt.

Weather Conditions:

- Sun
- Rain
- Fog
- Snow
- Freezing temperatures
- Wind

Sun

One of the most commonly overlooked weather conditions that impacts duck hunting is the sun. However, understanding how you can use the sun to your advantage can greatly improve your duck hunting success.

Two key points about sunny conditions:

- Looking directly into the sun makes it difficult for you to see ducks
- Ducks looking directly into the sun have a difficult time seeing you

If the wind conditions allow, it is good to set up in a spot where the sun will be at your back. This is because if you are looking over your spread, directly into the sun, it will make it particularly challenging to see approaching ducks. The sunrise and sunset times make it especially hard to see as the sun is right at eye level. Here is an example of the wind and sun being at the back of the hunter.

Duck Hunting Made Simple: 21 Steps to Duck Hunting Success

Not only will having the sun at your back make it easier for you to see approaching ducks, but it will also make it more difficult for ducks to see you as they approach your spread. Just as it is for humans, the sight of ducks is hindered by the bright light of the sun. If you force them to land as they look at the sun this will greatly reduce the chances of them spotting you, making it easier for you to bag more ducks.

Now you might be wondering, what to do if the wind and sun are coming from different directions. Well, that is a good question and often times that is the case where the wind and sun are not coming from the same direction and the good news there is still a way to use both the wind and sun to your benefit.

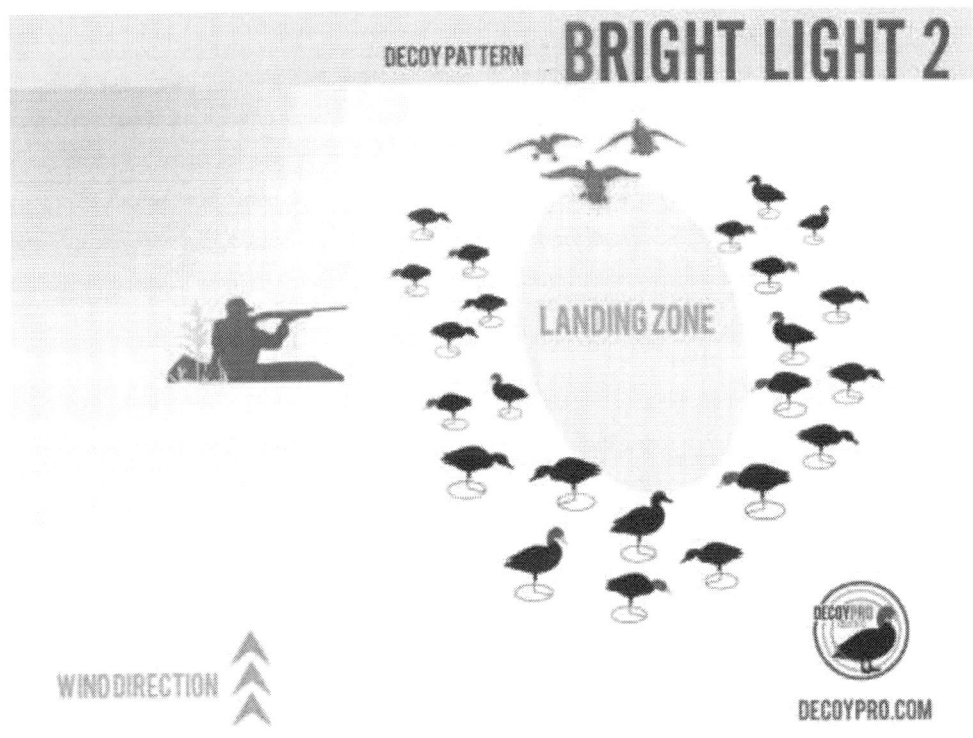

In this above example the hunter is hunting with a crosswind in a field. The wind is blowing from the bottom of the image up (north) so that means that the ducks will approach the spread from the top of the image (south). However, you can also see that the sun is coming from the left side of the image so the wind and sun are clearly not coming from the same direction.

This I not a problem because what we have done here is set the hunter to the outside part of the decoys with the decoys in a "U" shape in front of him. We have the opening of the "U" going with the wind to funnel the ducks in. The neat thing is that by placing the hunter off to the left is that as the ducks approach the spread and if they look his direction the sun will be at his back. By having the sun at his back it can help reduce the chances of him being spotted by the approaching ducks.

Rain

Chances are that if you hunt ducks or waterfowl there will be more than one occasion where you will encounter rain or storms during your outing. During these rainy days the vision of the ducks may be somewhat hindered depending on how hard the rain is coming down. One benefit to being out in the rain is that the ducks will have a harder time seeing you. In order for ducks to see your spread you will want to use your most visible decoys like oversized shell decoys or full body decoys if you have them.

Another benefit of hunting in the rain is that it can force ducks into more secluded areas. Finding one of these secluded locations could make for an incredibly fun day of bagging ducks even if you are getting rained on. This could be an area of the river or lake that has a lot of trees or other natural coverings that will keep the ducks out of the main path of any wind.

Fog

Hunting in fog can present some great opportunities for bagging waterfowl, including ducks. However, it will also present some challenges. One of the biggest benefits of hunting ducks in the fog is the fact that it will keep you out of sight of the ducks as they approach your spread. This can truly be a gift from Mother Nature as they will not see you until it is too late.

The downside is that hunting in fog will make it more difficult for the ducks to see your decoys. When in heavy fog, you may find the need to call more consistently for ducks than in clear conditions unless you are in a great location that ducks steadily land in. (More about calling in "Step 18 Duck Calling.") You will also want to use your most visible decoys in this weather. If you have oversized shell decoys these would work best.

Another challenge with hunting in the fog is that it can make it difficult for you to see and react to ducks before they are out of range. Ducks can quickly appear within your spread and before you ever have a chance to raise your gun, aim for an accurate shot and pull the trigger, the ducks may have already headed for safety. It will be important to stay on high alert the whole time you are hunting in fog if you want a good chance of bagging ducks.

Snow

Depending on the area that you hunt and how late into the season you chase birds, there is a chance that you will encounter snow. Similar to hunting in fog and rain, hunting when it is snowing can help keep you concealed from ducks as the flakes can hinder their sight. However, like I discussed with fog, it will also hinder your sight as the hunter so there may be a chance that ducks appear and disappear before you are able to react and shoot them.

It is also important to note that silhouette decoys can work well in snow over full body or shell decoys as the latter can collect snow on their backs making them disappear altogether or at least appear unrealistic. This does not mean that you cannot use full body decoys or shell decoys, just be prepared to get out of your hunting spot several times and head out into your spread to brush off any snow that has collected on their backs.

Freezing Temperatures

If you are getting to the point in the season where much of the water in the area has frozen over, this will narrow down the ducks' choice of locations as they will head for non-frozen water. This means that if you can locate a flowing part of a river or an area on a large body of water that is not frozen, you are likely to be in for a good day of hunting. Another thing you may notice in extreme temperatures is ducks may hold tight later into the morning before flying. If you normally see ducks fly within the first ½ hour you may now notice it take another hour or two before they get active.

Wind

Although I already discussed the impact of wind on decoy setup earlier in this book, it is important to bring it up again as part of this discussion about how weather impacts duck hunting. It is important to remember that ducks and almost all waterfowl will land into the wind. This is to assist them in making a gentle landing because they use the natural lift created by the wind during their descent.

In general you DO want to have some type of wind when you are duck hunting, as this will make planning your decoy setup much easier being that you can predict the direction that the ducks will come from. In contrast, days with little to no wind can pose a challenge as the direction the ducks will come from will be unpredictable.

Another thing to note is that if you own windsock decoys you would not be able to use these on a day with no wind as they rely on wind to fill the bodies and look lifelike. There are some types that have a backbone and don't require wind to fill their bodies so if you own that type you should be okay, but otherwise these will not be usable.

Now let's look at how to hide from the ducks…

Step 15: Concealing Yourself from the Ducks

Ensuring You're Properly Hidden from the Ducks

Many duck hunters do not conceal themselves well enough and it greatly impacts their ability to be successful. After all, if the approaching ducks see you they are not going to come within effective shotgun range. Blinds are a great way to conceal yourself from the ducks. I will discuss situations where you can hunt without a blind, but first I will look at the different types of blinds that can be used when needed. I will also then discuss some options of where to position yourself when hunting to help with concealment. (Also see "Step 17 Hunting Without Decoys" for a discussion on ways to conceal yourself when hunting without decoys.)

Types of blinds:

- Permanent water blinds
- Boat blinds
- Layout blinds
- Pit Blinds

Permanent Water Blinds

These types of blinds are often built to be season-long hunting spots. People make these out of a variety of materials ranging from wood to metal or anything else they have easy access to. It's best to use natural materials found in the area or at least mix these in. Typically they are built along the side of a pond, river or lake in a location where ducks like to land and fly over often.

If you are lucky enough to own hunting land with a body of water or have permanent access to land with water then you might consider investing the time and money into one of these blinds. As I mentioned, these can be made out of a variety of materials and it's really best to use what is naturally occurring in the area so the cost remains low. One nice thing with the permanent water blinds is that you can make them any size and shape you want. Many people make these to hold at least a few hunters and possibly a dog. This gives you a fun space to enjoy with fellow hunters on a consistent basis during the hunting season.

Boat Blinds

If you want to hunt in the middle of lakes or other bodies of water you will have to use a boat to get close enough to ducks to hunt them and you will need to hide it in order to keep from being seen. Hunting ducks from a boat is a truly unique experience so if you have the opportunity to try it, I would encourage you to do so.

Using a boat blind is one way to keep your boat hidden. A boat blind is a structure available for purchase to go over your boat and is usually a metal frame with nylon camouflage material. You can enhance these by adding tall grass or reed coverings and looping these through the sides and/or draping them over the top of the blind.

You can also make a boat blind yourself or just use the tall grass and reed coverings to drape over the sides and top of your boat itself. You can purchase fake grass and reed-type material from a hunting or outdoor store if you do not want to spend the time gathering the naturally-occurring material in the area each time you hunt from a boat. If you are not in the middle of the water and want to hunt near the shore with your boat, you can just conceal yourself in the naturally-occurring vegetation along the side without actually covering your boat.

Layout Blinds

A layout blind is a type of blind that lies on the ground and usually has a built-in reclining seat. It typically has two flaps or doors that you pull down to cover up. Once ducks come in range you pop the flaps/doors open and shoot. These blinds are most often used if you are field hunting for ducks but can also be used on the shore of a body of water.

These really can make for an enjoyable hunt as you get to lie back and wait for the ducks to come. I would recommend looking for one with a good amount of padding on the backrest for those days that you plan to be there for several hours. Most of these blinds are waterproof up to a certain level of water. For example, some are rated for 3 inches of water meaning you could actually set your blind in 3 inches of standing water and the water would not get into the blind. Expect to pay $125-$350 for a quality new layout blind.

It's important to note that if you do purchase a new blind you will want to break it in by "mudding" it first so that it looks more natural and blends in better. To do this you will want to mix up a bucket of mud and take an old mop or paint brush and cover your blind with the mixture. Let the mud dry and then shake or sweep it off. Doing this helps take some of the shine from the brand new paint off and helps it blend in better. This is called "mudding your blind."

When setting up your blind, particularly if it is in the open, you will first want to survey the area and see what type of natural covering you have to assist in concealment.

What you can use to conceal your blind:

- Tall grasses or reeds on the edge of crop fields or on the shore of bodies of water
- Corn or other crops not yet harvested, missed, or lying on the ground of fields you are hunting
- Fake covering purchased at a hunting store

Most hunting blinds have loops all over them that are specifically designed to allow you to weave natural covering within them. These loops are very handy as they are all over the blind so you can loop the concealment covering over every place of the blind to help your blind blend in naturally with the surroundings.

One thing you want to pay attention to when covering your blind is to not take too much covering from one area. In other words, you do not want to take all of the downed corn stalks that are right by your hunting blind. If you do this it will actually make your blind stick out like a sore thumb because the area will be clear and then you will have a big pile of corn stalks all in one place. It is best to walk a good distance away (20-30 yards) from your blind to gather up material and bring it back to your hunting blind.

Pit Blinds

A pit blind is a type of blind that goes in the ground. These can simply be a hole dug in the ground and concealed with natural covering that you can find in the area, or they can be more elaborate structures made of wood, steel or fiberglass. They can be built right in the hole in the ground or they can be purchased and a hole dug to fit them. These are fairly permanent structures and usually need to be covered when not in use. You will probably only have the opportunity to use one of these if you are hunting on your own property or have gotten permission to build one on someone else's property.

Positioning Yourself

There are several options of where to position yourself when hunting ducks to help with concealment.

Options of where to position yourself:

- Within the decoy spread (if you are using decoys)
- In the natural covering on the shore of a body of water or on the edge of a field
- In the rows of remaining crops on a partially-harvested corn field (or other crop field with tall enough crops to hide in) – usually want to be 2-3 rows back

Within the Decoy Spread

One option of where to position yourself when hunting is within the decoy spread (if you are using decoys). This is advantageous as the decoys can help conceal you from the view of the ducks. You just have to be careful of being in their direct line of view as this can lead to you being spotted and scaring them off. This is a situation where you would most likely want to use a blind and conceal it well with naturally-occurring or store-bought vegetation.

Here is an example of hunting within the spread:

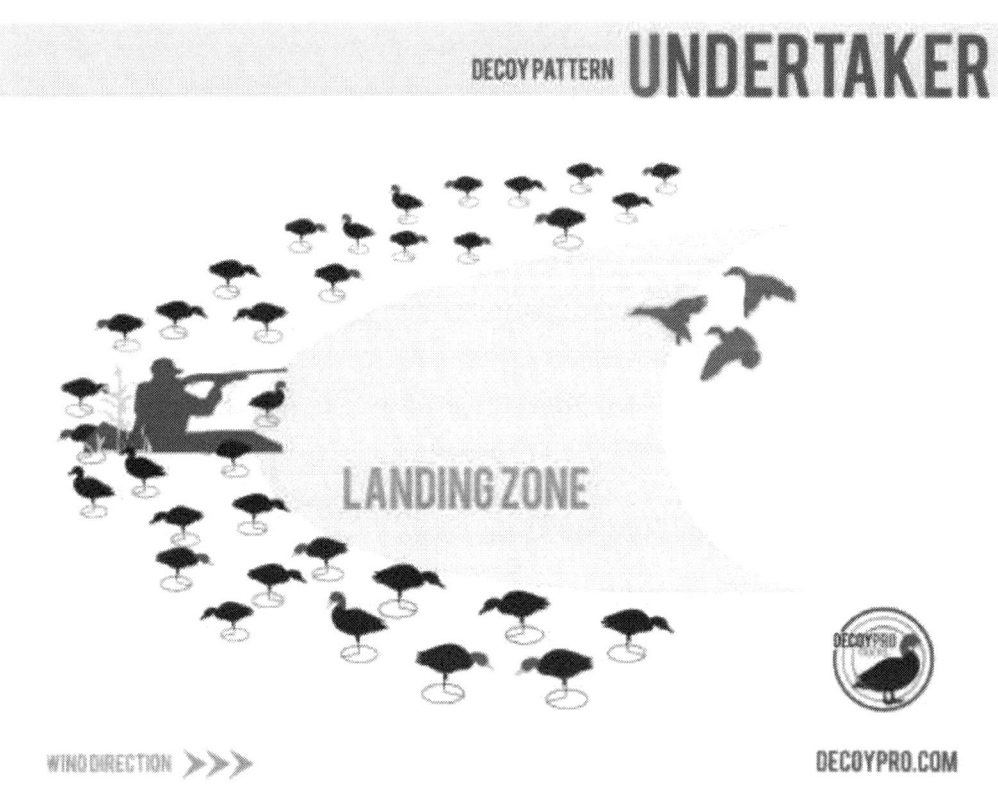

If hunting in the middle of a harvested crop field, when you set up you want to be parallel to the chopped rows of crops. This helps to reduce the visual impact that you will have on approaching ducks. If you place yourself and/or your blind across the rows of crops it will make you stick out more to ducks, likely leading them to fly off before you have a chance to shoot them. You would want to factor this in before setting up your decoys as this would determine the direction you lay them out. Of course since you also have to take wind direction and sun into consideration (as I will discuss later) it might not be possible to set up in the direction of the crops.

In the Natural Covering on the Shore of a Body of Water or on the Edge of a Field

The tall grass on the side of a pond or other body of water provides a good spot in which the hunter can set up. You can hunt in this situation without a blind as you can just use the natural covering alone to conceal yourself. You can put some of the natural covering over yourself for additional concealment. As long as you are wearing camouflage clothing you should be concealed well from the approaching ducks. The tall grass on the edge of a field can also be used in the same way and should be enough to conceal you without the need for a blind.

Here is an example of hunting with the natural coverings on a shore:

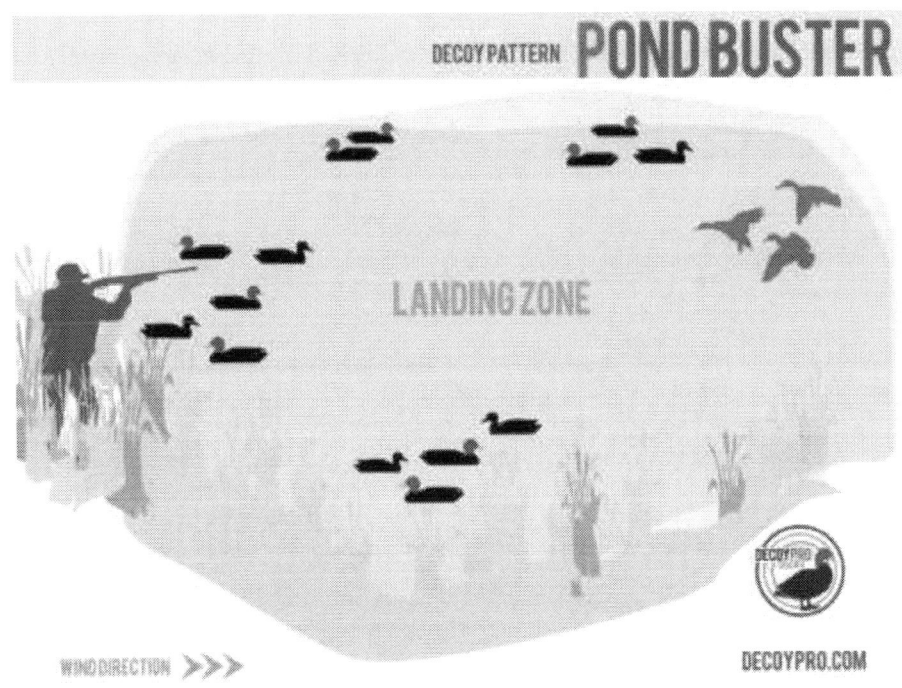

In the Remaining Rows of Crops on a Partially-Harvested Field

Many times farmers will cut down a portion of their field and leave another portion of the crops in the field standing. Farmers will do this for a few reasons including: running out of time and planning to come back later to finish; giving a portion of the crops time to further grow or dry out before they harvest them all; being required to leave a few rows of standing crop for insurance purposes. Regardless of the reason it is a great place to hide.

Usually this works best with a corn field as that crop is tall enough to hide in. You can use this option when there are remaining crops next to an open, harvested part of the field where you can hope for ducks to land. You would want to position yourself 2-3 rows back in the crop. If you are hunting with decoys you would want to leave 15-20 yards between the crops and your spread because ducks would not naturally land right next to standing crops as they would be wary of predators. Again, this is a situation where you would not need a blind in order to be hidden from the ducks.

Here is an example of hunting in standing corn:

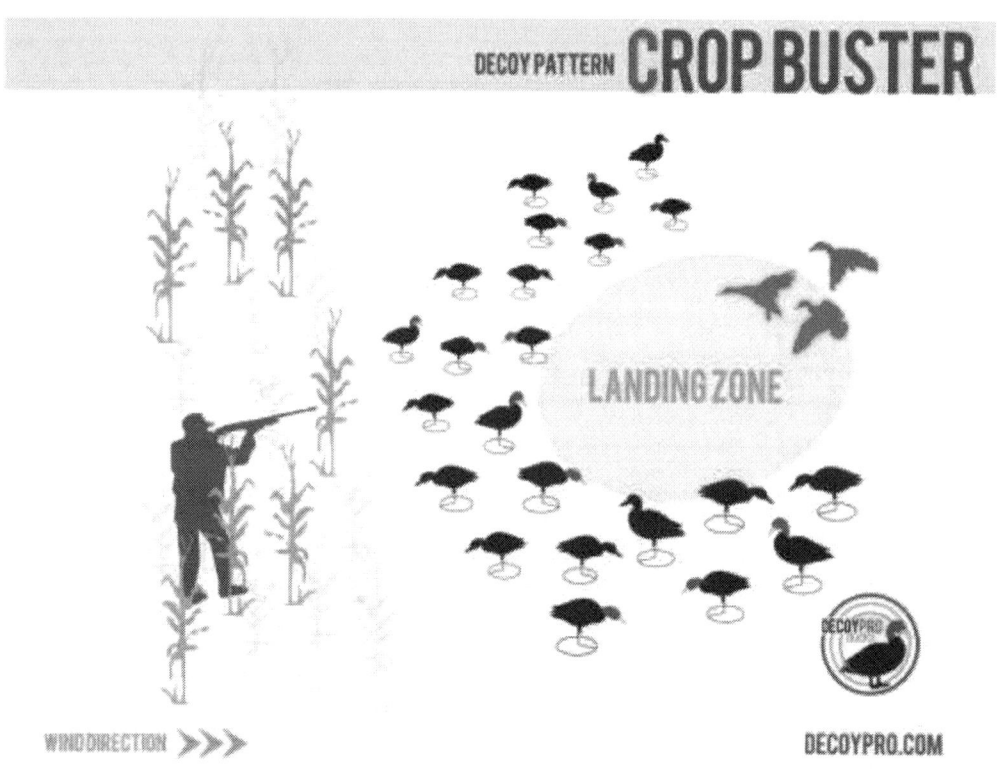

Summary

If you have a permanent water or pit blind available for use and/or want or need to hunt out in the open (in the field or on water) then a blind is a great option. Just remember to conceal it well and/or use your decoy spread to help with cover. However, if you don't have a permanent blind, hunting without a blind can be a lot easier and require a lot less effort. So take advantage of one of the situations above that provide natural cover if you can.

Now let's find out how to set up decoys to attract ducks most effectively…

Step 16: Decoy Setup and Adjustment

Placing Decoys Can Be Easy

With just a few tips that are given here you will be able to successfully set up your duck decoys and instantly improve your success. In addition to these tips I also provide several easy-to-read diagrams of effective decoy spreads, showing you exactly how to position your decoys in order to attract and shoot ducks.

Critical components to hunting with decoys:

- Proper distance between decoys
- Facing the decoys the right direction
- Proper shooting distance to landing zone
- Use of effective decoy spreads such as: the "Undertaker," the "Vaporizer," the "Shore Slayer," the "Xtreme," and the "Ring of Fire"
- Incorporating confidence decoys
- Adjusting your spread when necessary

Distance Between Decoys

When setting up duck decoys try to leave about 5-8 feet in between your decoys. If you watch ducks land naturally you will see that they do not land right on top of each other. It is important to reproduce a real-life situation with your decoy spread which is why you need to leave space between your decoys. If you put your decoys too close together you may notice that ducks will fly over your decoy spread but never end up landing because they feel crowded.

When setting up in a field I recommend setting one decoy down and then taking two large steps and putting your next decoy down. With each step you should move about 2-3 feet so two large steps in between decoys will leave you with appropriate distance in between your decoys.

Decoy Facing

Ducks do not all feed or sit facing the same direction. As you set up your decoys, randomly face them in all different directions. It is okay to have a few that are facing the same direction but you typically do not want all of them facing one direction. Pay attention to ducks that you see in fields and ponds and you will notice that they are all facing different directions. You will only have to worry about decoys you place on land as those you place in water will move with the motion of the wind and current and end up facing random directions anyway.

Shooting Distance

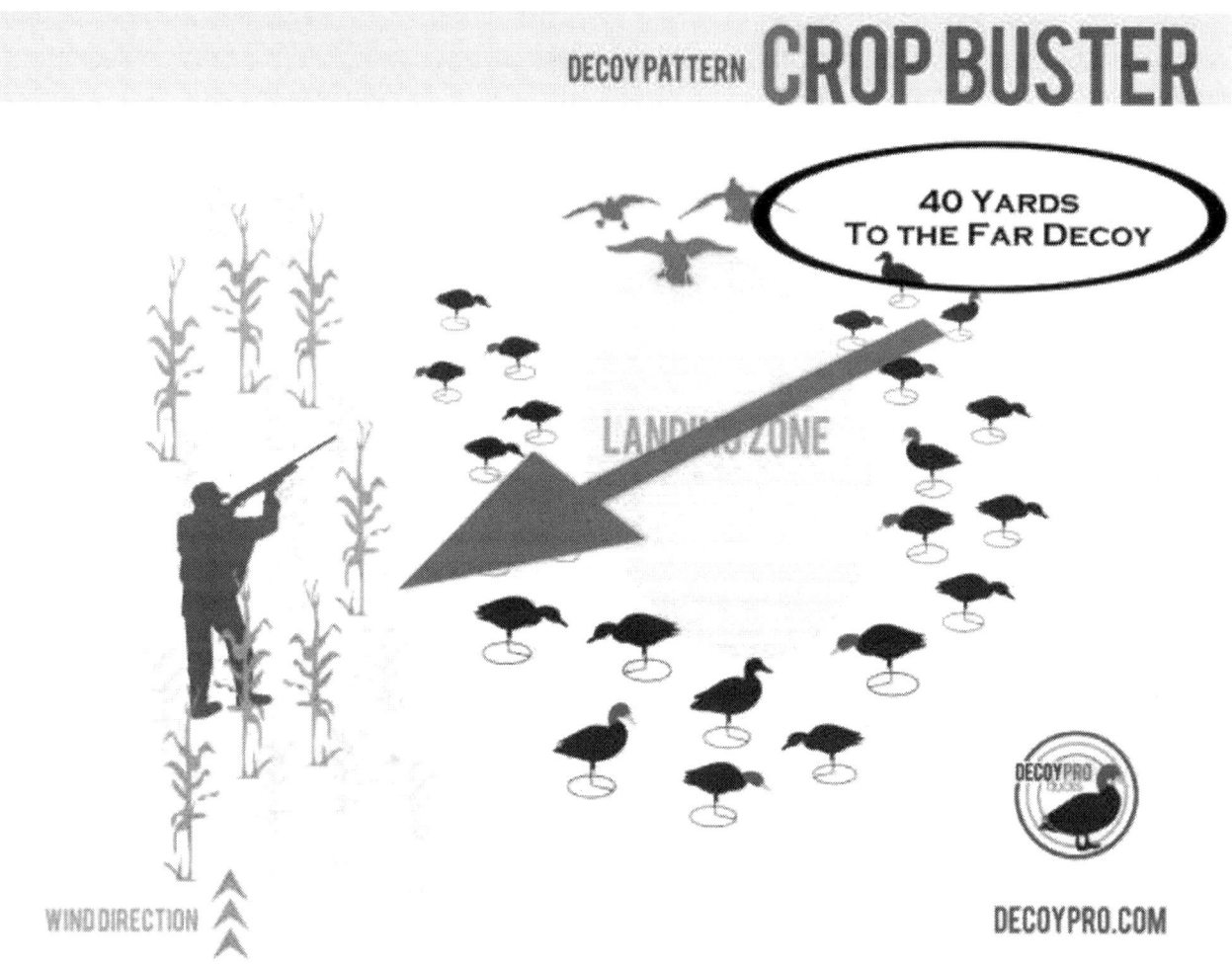

When you set up your decoys you want to pay attention to how far you will be sitting from the furthest point in the landing zone. This is because shotguns have an effective range of about 40 yards. If you set up your decoys in a manner where much of the landing zone is more than 40 yards away, this can lead to ducks coming in but you never having a chance to shoot them because they are outside of shotgun range.

Common Decoy Spreads

Now I will show you some common decoy spreads that you can use. As you will see some are on water and some on land. And some can be used for both.

The "Undertaker" (or "U") Over Water (also known as the "Splash Zone")

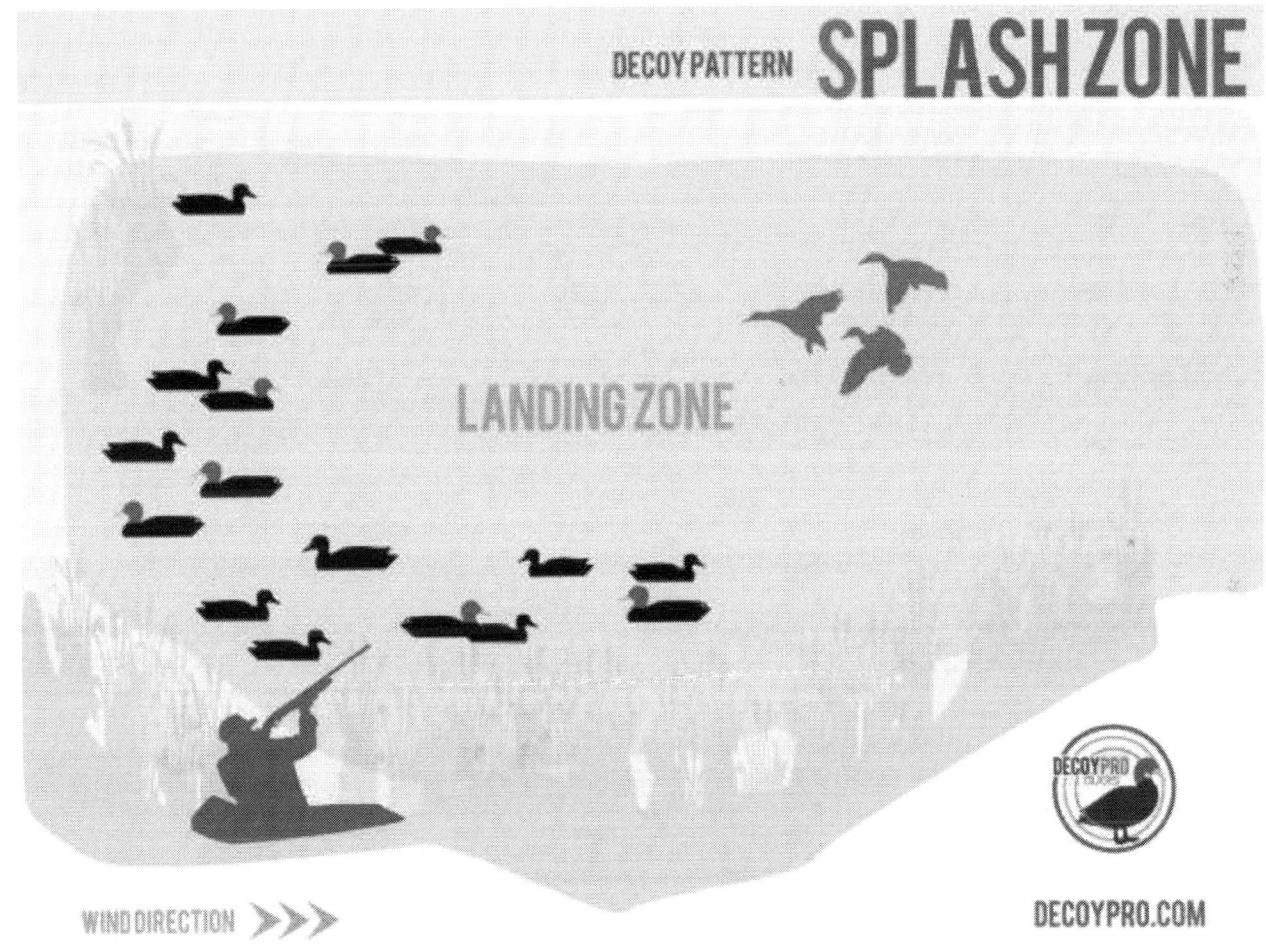

This decoy setup technique funnels ducks into the opening of a "U" shape. This is a great method to use when you have a strong wind coming consistently from one direction. In this example the hunter is positioned on the side of the water as there is natural covering available there. He could also position himself at the base of the "U" and use any natural cover there or use decoys as cover. When sitting at the base, if there is no natural cover, you will most likely want to use a blind as the ducks will be looking directly at your location when they fly in.

The "Undertaker" (or "U") On a Field

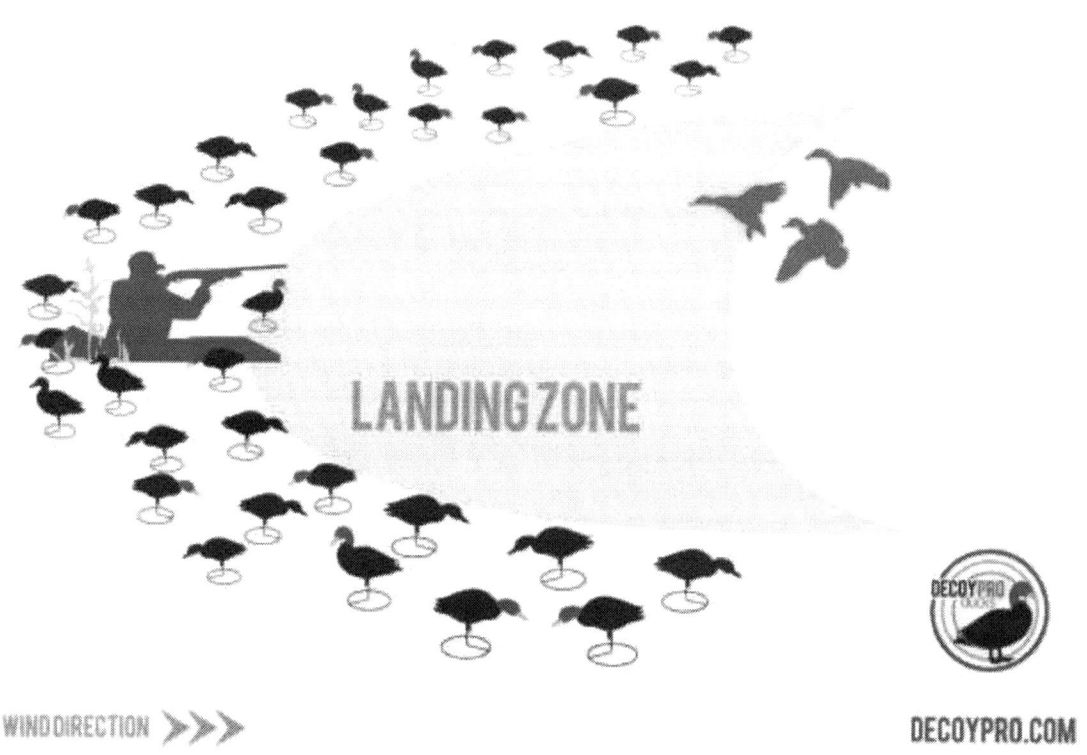

The same setup pattern can also be used in a field and this example shows the hunter positioned within the decoys as there is no natural covering to hide in on the sides of the spread.

"Undertaker" (or "U") summary:

- Easy decoy setup to learn for beginners
- Good when wind direction is consistent
- Funnels ducks to provide "in-your-face" shooting

- Great for single hunter
- Can support more hunters if you increase decoy spread size
- Can be set up with as few as 12-18 decoys

The "Vaporizer" (or "V")

The "Vaporizer" is also a great method to use when you have a strong wind coming consistently from one direction and is an easy setup to remember when placing decoys in the field. In fact it is a similar spread to the "Undertaker" with a more pronounced line of decoys jutting out.

For a single hunter this can be used with as few as 12-18 decoys. With multiple hunters you will want to use more decoys to ensure there are enough decoys to conceal each blind. To accommodate multiple hunters you would just widen the base of the "V."

"Vaporizer" (or "V") summary:

- Easy decoy setup to learn
- Good when wind direction is consistent
- Can be used with one or multiple hunters depending on number of decoys
- Direct shooting opportunities
- Large landing zone
- Can be set up with as few as 12-18 decoys for a single hunter

Duck Hunting Made Simple: 21 Steps to Duck Hunting Success

The "Shore Slayer"

The "Shore Slayer' is a similar setup to the "U" with the intent of funneling ducks into a landing zone in the middle section of the decoys. The "Shore Slayer" spread is commonly used when hunting ducks along rivers or large lakes. Sometimes people leave a space between a few of the decoys in the spread as an escape route for the ducks. Ducks do not always like to fly over other ducks so this leaves an escape path they can take without going around the spread. If they take this escape route you still have a chance for pass shooting. (More about pass shooting in "Step 20 Shooting.")

The "Shore Slayer" is a great option when hunting shorelines of larger bodies of water such as lakes and even oceans. With the "Shore Slayer" you make a long line of decoys about 30 yards out from the shore. Then you put another smaller group of decoys near the shoreline creating a small opening in between the two groups of decoys as outlined in the diagram.

"Shore Slayer" summary:

- Funnels ducks into a specific landing zone
- Easy setup to learn
- The long line of decoys creates a barrier to stop passing by flocks
- Use when wind direction is consistent with minor direction changes
- Large landing zone
- Works well for large bodies of water
- Close shooting as ducks travel the shoreline
- Opening in between the decoy groups makes the ducks flying through feel comfortable
- Use the natural covering on the shore to hide

The "Xtreme" (or "X")

The "Xtreme" is one of the most versatile decoy spreads because the "X" setup provides 4 landing zones. This design has a very unique advantage because it works regardless of the wind direction. This can be used on land or water. If the wind changes direction after you set up your decoys all you need to do is turn the direction your blind (or boat) is facing. This setup also works when there is little or no wind. To effectively setup this spread you will need at least 3-4 dozen decoys.

On more than one occasion I have set up decoys in the morning with the wind blowing one direction only to later to have the wind completely change directions. This is very frustrating when you have to change your decoy spread. I have also had days where ducks seem to want to land at a slightly different angle that what I was anticipating. The great thing with the "X" is you are covered in all directions. If the wind changes all you have to do is simply change the direction that your blind or boat is facing and you will be in perfect position for any approaching ducks.

The one downside of this spread is that you will need a larger number of decoys. With the "U" or "V" you only have two long lines of decoys heading out from the starting point of the spread; however, with the "X" you have 4 long points coming off of the center of the "X" so you will need to have a sufficient amount of decoys to make these lines.

"Xtreme" (or "X") summary:

- Multiple landing zones
- Use when wind direction is rapidly changing
- Effective on no wind days
- Eliminates need to adjust decoys
- Requires several dozen decoys (40+ decoys)

The "Ring of Fire"

The "Ring of Fire" setup gets ducks to land in the opening of a circle. This design helps to get ducks to drop into a very specific spot on the field allowing the hunter to find a great spot to set up the blind in close proximity to the landing zone. The circle should be about 40 yards across. Again, this setup is good for when the wind is changing directions or when there is no wind as the hunter can easily reposition himself on another part of the circle to adjust for how birds are landing.

"Ring of Fire" summary:

- Large landing zone with a 40 yard circumference
- Easy hunter relocation if wind changes
- Works on days with no wind
- Directs ducks into a very specific landing location
- Requires a few dozen decoys

Incorporating "Confidence" Decoys

I discussed earlier in the book that including a few other species of birds with your duck decoys can add an additional level of realism to your spread and help it stand out. In this case I have added some floating goose decoys to the edges of the spread. This will help increase the visibility of your spread to ducks and it may help you get some geese to shoot as well. Particularly in the later season when ducks have seen a lot of hunting pressure, the addition of confidence decoys can sometimes be just enough to entice the ducks to come in for a landing.

Adjusting Your Spread When Necessary

It is inevitable that on at least one of your hunts the wind will change direction after you have set up your decoys. On more than one occasion I have spent over an hour setting up my decoys only to then have the wind change direction. I showed you some examples above of spreads that are flexible enough to allow for changing wind direction; however, if you are not using one of these spreads you will want to know how to adjust your spread when necessary.

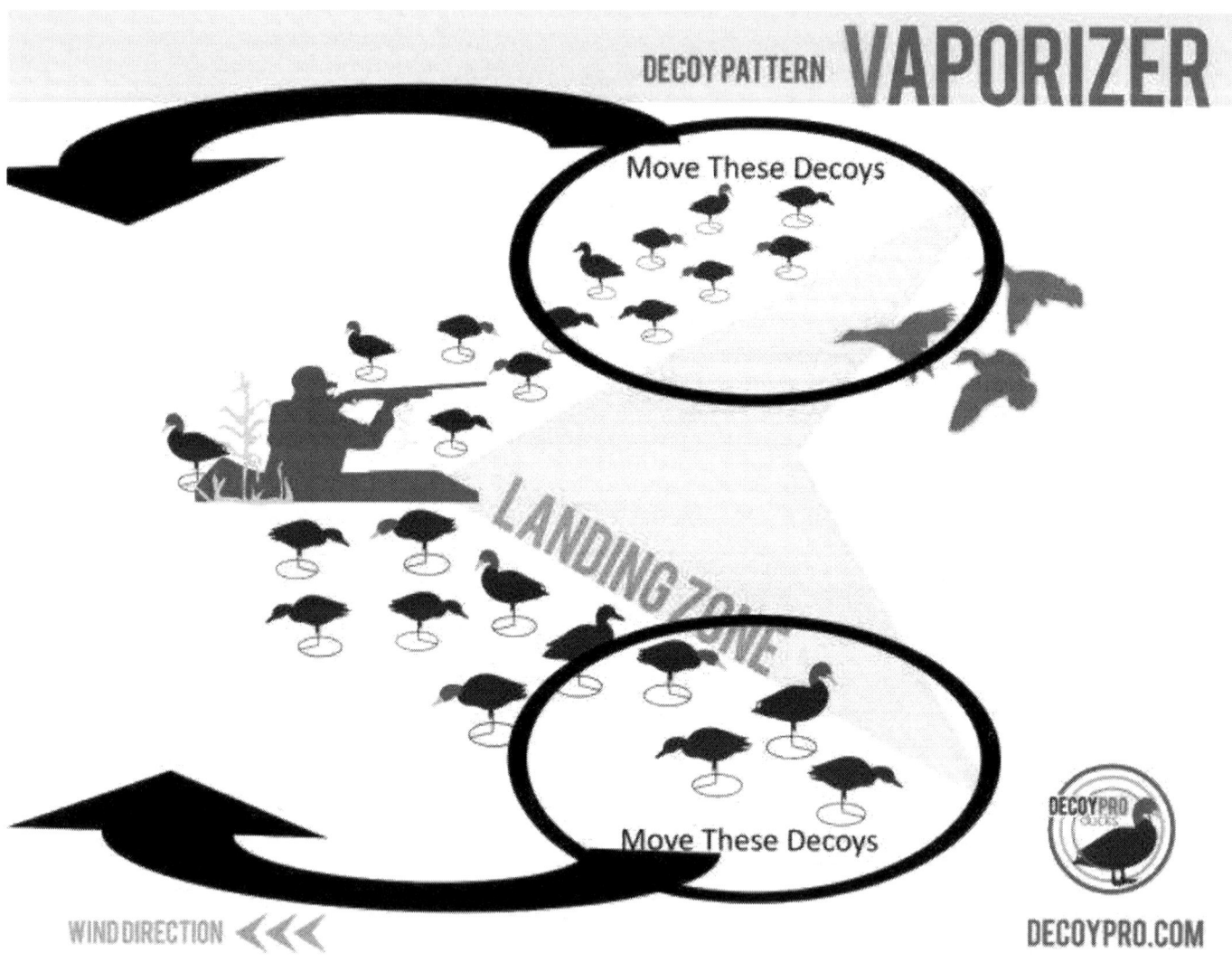

As frustrating as it can be to have to adjust your spread, there is a way you can minimize the amount of time that it will take you to adjust your decoys by using the 80/20 rule. Essentially, with the 80/20 rule you leave 80 percent of your decoys in the same spot where you set them up and you only move 20 percent of your decoys. See the above diagram on how to accomplish this task quickly. The 80/20 rule allows me to make spread adjustments in about 5-10 minutes compared to 30 minutes or more if I were to move all of the decoys.

In addition to wind changing direction, ducks may react differently than what you anticipate. If you notice that ducks will not land in your spread, it is a good idea to make quick adjustments. Personally, I would rather change up my spread type quickly than waste an entire day in the field with ducks flying by and not landing in my spread.

Final Review of Decoy Setup

What I showed you in this section are some general guidelines for decoy setup. Pay attention to how the ducks are reacting to what you have set up and do not be afraid to make adjustments if ducks are not landing. There are many more spread types that you can learn about in books or online so continue to note what you have success with and learn from each hunting trip.

Now let's discuss hunting ducks without decoys...

Step 17: Hunting Without Decoys

Can I Be Successful Without Decoys?

People regularly ask if it is possible to hunt ducks without decoys and the short answer is "yes." However, to have success hunting ducks without decoys you will need to plan your hunt even better than if you had decoys and be prepared to possibly experience more difficult shooting.

Critical components to hunting without decoys:

- Identify bodies of water and fields used by ducks
- Hunter concealment
- Find a funnel
- Pass shooting

Identify Bodies of Water and Fields Used by Ducks

It is particularly important when hunting ducks without decoys to locate where ducks are. Look for the bodies of water and fields where ducks are seen regularly. I am lucky enough to be able to hunt my father-in-law's land that has a small pond near a river where ducks regularly hang out. Although there are times when I do put out a few decoys in this pond, there are many times where it is not even necessary to have decoys out. The ducks frequent this pond so regularly in the early season that I do not need decoys to attract them.

This is the time where you will really need to invest some time in driving around and finding the spots where ducks are feeding and resting. If you drive by a field and see dozens of ducks feeding there this is probably going to be a good spot to hunt as long as you can get there for the hunt within a day or two. Ducks do change their flight and feeding patterns but if you see ducks in a location in an afternoon and you can return to that same spot to hunt the next morning you should be in for some pretty good hunting even without decoys.

Hunter Concealment

In addition to the need to locate bodies of water and fields ahead of time that are frequented by ducks when not using decoys, you will also need to plan your concealment method better as you will not have the decoy spread to help with concealment. Layout blinds are not as effective without decoys as they stand out more to approaching ducks than they would if you had decoys all around them. If you have natural covering in which to help conceal a layout blind, it can still be used, or if you have a permanent water or pit blind you can always use these without decoys; however, below are ways you can conceal yourself without decoys or a blind.

How to conceal yourself when hunting without decoys or a blind:

- Hide in standing crops or any other natural cover available
- Sit at fence line
- Sit at the tree line
- Lie in the field and cover with downed crops

If there is standing corn or other crops near where the ducks are landing you can hide in the crops. You can also use any other natural vegetation such as tall grasses next to fields or on the shores of water to hide in if they are close by where ducks are landing.

If there is no natural cover available you can do one of three things: sit at a fence line, sit at a tree line, or lie in the field. If you sit near a fence or tree line this should make you less visible to the ducks flying over. Lying in the field exactly where the ducks are landing is a good technique as long as you do not mind getting a little dirty. To do this effectively you will want to use some of the surrounding crops for cover. For example, if you are hunting a chopped cornfield there will most likely be some downed stalks that the combine did not pick up. Gather some of these up then lie down and cover yourself as best as possible. When the ducks come in to land you should be able to quickly pop up and get some good shooting in.

Find a Funnel

One great way to hunt ducks without decoys is to find a funnel where ducks are forced to fly through a tight area. For example, hunting a river that has high trees and grass on both sides can be a great option. This is because ducks will fly up and down the river in between the trees which will keep them in close enough range to get great shooting in from the riverbank.

Pass Shooting

When hunting ducks without decoys the majority of your shooting will likely be done as pass shooting. What this means is that you will be shooting at ducks flying past rather than at ducks preparing to land or already landed as you are usually doing when you use decoys. We will cover shooting techniques later, but just be aware that the difficulty level will usually be increased if you elect to hunt ducks without decoys.

Now let's discuss how to pull ducks into range by calling…

Step 18: Duck Calling

Using a Duck Call Can Be Very Effective

A great way to get attention from nearby ducks is to use a duck call. Once you learn how to effectively call ducks, you can typically get ducks to come to your spread that would have otherwise flown past. This can help you greatly improve the amount of ducks you bag on each of your hunting trips.

Considerations for calling ducks:

- Types of duck calls
- Call sounds and timing
- How to learn more about calling
- Calling is not always necessary

Types of Duck Calls

Duck calls are typically made out of wood or hard plastic acrylic material and can range from $20-$200. However there are a wide variety of duck calls on the market. If you go to any local sporting goods store you can look around and see what you like best as well ask for some recommendations from the store associates. Many stores will actually let you test a few calls so you can see what type you like before you buy.

Types of duck calls:

- Single Reed- the loudest of the duck calls; great for advanced callers
- Double Reed- usually the easiest for beginners to learn

Call Sounds and Timing

Pay attention to your specific situation when calling for ducks. The ducks' location and their behavior will impact what type of call sound you should make.

Common Duck Call Sounds:

- **Quack**- This is a loud call used to get the attention of the ducks from a distance. Say "wit" repeatedly into the call.
- **Feeding**- After you have the attention of ducks use this call to keep them interested. Say "ticka" several times with your hands cupped around the call and one hand slightly open.
- **Comeback**- If ducks fly over your spread but don't seem committed you can try the comeback call. A word regularly used to get this sound is "kanc."

How to Learn to Call Ducks

We have covered just the very basics of duck call sounds. Entire books have been written on this topic and to be honest it is something that is difficult to teach in a book compared to videos and practice. To learn more about duck calling try some of the following resources. Also note that instructions come with the purchase of a duck call.

Where to learn more about calling:

- CDs sold at hunting stores
- YouTube videos. Search "how to call ducks"
- Online hunting forums
- Other hunters
- Books
- Practice

It is my recommendation to practice duck calling quite a bit at home prior to using the call in the field. Buy yourself a duck call and then spend 15 minutes a day for at least month leading up to the hunting season. 15 minutes a day will go a long way towards how to learn to call and after a month of practice you should at least be able to make the basic sounds to attract ducks. Please note that it can take years to become a really good caller so do not get discouraged at first. Learning how to call is just like anything else, at first it can be challenging but the more you practice the easier it will get.

Calling is Not Always Necessary

I also want to point out that it is not always necessary to call for ducks. If you have ducks that are visibly locked into your decoy spread just let them come. Sometimes overcalling can actually scare ducks away. I like to mention this because there are some people who think they must master calling before they can go duck hunting; however, this is simply not true. In fact, the majority of ducks I have shot have been without any calling at all. If you use all of the tips I provided earlier in this book you can have plenty of success without calling ducks.

Here are some other ways to get the attention of ducks...

Step 19: Other Attention-Grabbing Techniques

What Other Ways Can I Get a Duck's Attention?

We already know that decoy spreads are used to get the attention of ducks. We also know that if there is movement in the spread created by various means such as stands, motion stakes, spinning wing decoys or windsock decoys that ducks will be more likely to come. We also just discussed how calling can get the attention of ducks. A few more tricks to try would be using duck flags or jerk strings.

This section covers:

- Duck Flags
- Jerk Strings
- Swimming Decoys
- Spinning Wing Decoy Spread Tips

Duck Flags

Duck flags are pretty simple in design and are made to imitate the look of flapping wings of ducks. They come on plastic handles and the wing is usually made out of thin plastic or fabric mimicking a duck's wing. The flag mimics the ducks wing because the colors of the duck you are hunting are painted on the fabric of the flag. You simply wave your arm up and down at a 45 degree angle when ducks are in the distance to grab their attention. These are very inexpensive and can usually be purchased brand new for about $20. I would consider this a very cheap way to get the attention of passing ducks.

Typically, you would only use the ducks when they are a distance of several hundred yards away and most often these are used when field hunting ducks. You use these to try and grab the attention of any flocks of ducks that are out in the distance and may not see your decoy spread. You can actually stand up and walk into your decoys and waive the flag when the ducks are a long ways away for added visibility. However, once they turn your direction you will want to quickly head to your hunting blind to avoid being spotted.

Jerk Strings

A jerk string is a string that are attached to a line of duck decoys in the water. When you pull the string it makes the decoys move back and forth creating ripples in the water to catch the eye of passing ducks. Again, the intent is to trick the ducks into thinking that your decoys are real ducks because real ducks do not sit still when they are in the water. These can be particularly effective when hunting areas like flooded timber because as the ducks fly over the decoys can sometimes be difficult for the ducks to see. However, by adding some movement it can catch the attention of passing by ducks from further away.

Swimming Decoys

In addition to the spinning wing decoys that we discussed earlier that are elevated above the land or water and have moving wings to grab the attention of ducks, there are also swimming decoys for water use. Some of these have wings that spin around in circles like a spinning wing decoy and as the wings spin they cause water to get splashed up into the air.

There are also some models of these decoys that make the decoys vibrate and move back and forth in a similar manner to what a jerk string would do. However, these are typically battery powered so you do not have to use your arms to create the motion and that frees up your hands to shoot ducks as they approach.

Spinning Wing Decoy Spread Tips

One more attention grabbing technique that I want to share is the utilization of spinning wing decoys. In step 5 I gave an overview of this decoy but as a reminder a spinning wing decoy is a decoy that has wings that spin in circles to create the look that a duck is landing. Implementing a few of these into your decoy spread can be one of the absolute best ways to pull in nearby ducks. What I would like to do now is give you a few tips on using these decoys so let me start by showing you an example setup that incorporates a spinning wing decoy.

Duck Hunting Made Simple: 21 Steps to Duck Hunting Success

The first tip I want to give you about the spinning wing decoys is I recommend placing the decoys so they are facing into your decoy spread. As you can see in this example I have the spinning wing decoys head facing towards the majority of the decoys in the landing zone to recreate the appearance that a duck is landing. This is a natural look because ducks will land into the wind so having the decoys head facing into the wind is realistic.

Additionally, I like to have the spinning wing decoys towards the front portion of the spread. What I mean is I like to have them closer to the landing zone rather than further into the spread. Approaching ducks will often land close to the spinning wing decoys so by putting these decoys close to the landing zone it will help direct those ducks to the place where I want them so I have easy and close shooting opportunities.

Another tip to share is placing the decoy off to the side of your hunting spot. If you look at the example you can see that I have the spinning wing decoy slightly off to the left side of the location where the hunter is positioned and I do this for two reasons. First, the approaching ducks will often be focusing their attention at the spinning wing decoys. This means if my hunting spot is right behind where the decoy is placed it may increase my chances of being spotted by the ducks since they will be looking right where I'm sitting.

In addition, I like having the decoy slightly to the side so that it is not in my direct shooting path. If the decoy was right in front of me it would hinder many of my shooting opportunities as ducks approach or I might accidentally hit the decoy with a shot. These decoys are not cheap so by setting it off to the side I still accomplish my goal of attracting ducks but I also accomplish my goal of having clear and close shooting paths towards any approaching ducks.

Now let's discuss how to shoot ducks once you draw them in…

Step 20: Shooting

Ducks Are in Sight – How Do You Shoot Them?

When you finally have ducks within shooting range it is the most exciting part of your duck hunting trip. My heart races every time I see ducks approach my hunting spot. I hope that through the tips I provide you in this book you are able to experience this feeling many times over. Use the following shooting tips to make the most out of your shooting opportunities once these ducks are in range.

Shooting tips:

- Practice in advance
- Watch for "cupped wings"
- Lead your birds when pass shooting
- Use humane shooting practices and scare birds up when necessary
- Place your shot
- Learn from missed shots

Practice in Advance

Duck Hunting Made Simple: 21 Steps to Duck Hunting Success

If you have never been duck hunting or if you are having difficulty hitting ducks then it might be a good idea to get some target practice in before your next hunting trip. One of the easiest and most cost effective ways to practice shooting is to visit a gun club.

Chances are you live within a half hour of a gun club where you can pay a fee to shoot some clay pigeons. This is usually inexpensive as you can buy a round of 25 clay pigeons for about $8-$10 and a box of target shotgun shells for around $7 for a total of less than $20. This minimal investment could greatly improve your success on your next bird outing.

Watch for "Cupped Wings"

When you get ducks that are about to land they will get to the point where they cup their wings. They are prepping for a landing and are looking for a comfortable landing spot. This is one of the best times to shoot a duck if you don't believe in shooting them once they have landed. Just be sure they are within shooting range which is generally 40 yards. Some hunters will wait until they have actually landed to shoot but we will discuss that in a minute.

Lead Your Birds When Pass Shooting

Pass shooting is when you are shooting at birds that are flying by. Pass shooting is a very common practice with duck hunting as birds may be flying by your area as they go to their favorite feeding or resting spot or they may be flying by as they are checking out your spread or entering or leaving your spread. As I discussed earlier, if you do not use decoys most of your shooting will be done using this method as you are not enticing the birds to land.

For pass shooting it is important to lead your birds. What this means is that you do not want to aim directly at the body of the bird when you shoot. The reason this is ineffective is because ducks are so fast that if you aim directly at them by the time you pull the trigger and the BBs reach the area the duck was at you will have shot behind the duck. Follow the steps below to effectively shoot a duck that is flying by.

How to pass shoot:

1. Aim slightly ahead of the duck.
2. Pull the trigger.
3. Continue to move your gun in the path of the duck.
4. Take a second shot if necessary.

Humane Shooting Practices and Scaring Birds Up

There is some controversy in the waterfowl community concerning shooting birds that have landed. Some people are of the belief that shooting ducks when they have landed is unsportsmanlike because they feel the shooting is too easy and does not give the ducks a chance compared to when they are flying.

In contrast, others believe it is actually more humane to shoot ducks after they have landed because it is more likely that a quick and effective kill shot can be made in this situation compared to when the birds are in flight. So really it is up to the hunter and their beliefs how they handle this issue. Some also just like the greater challenge of shooting a bird in flight vs. when it is sitting on the ground or in the water. One option if you don't want to shoot a duck that has landed is to scare it back into flight.

If a duck has landed and you don't want to shoot it when it is not in flight, you can scare it back up by yelling "up" and then take your shot once it is back in the air. If you are okay with shooting it on the ground, again, just be sure it is within shooting range. If you see it is coming closer, wait until it is close as possible before shooting to get the best shot possible. Just keep in mind the longer you wait the more chance you have that it might take off again.

Place Your Shot

Now let's discuss where on the duck you should attempt to place your shot. If possible, the best place to hit the duck is in the head and chest area as an accurately-placed shot here will provide a very quick and lethal kill. This will also preserve the most meat. With a shotgun, since it produces multiple shots, it will be hard not to sometimes hit other parts of the body of the duck too, but at least if you aim for the head and chest you will be better off. In some cases the bird will be flying away from you so you have no other choice but to shoot it from behind. Just be aware that the thickest feathers are on the back side of the bird so when you are shooting them from behind they have the most protection from the BBs lowering the chance that the BBs will penetrate for a kill.

Learn From Missed Shots

Any duck hunter regardless of experience level has missed many shots so it is important to not let yourself get down when you miss. Use missed shot as an opportunity to learn from your mistakes. After more time hunting your hit rates will improve but keep in mind that you will never have 100% accuracy and that is completely normal.

Keep reading to learn how to clean the ducks you just shot…

Step 21: Duck Cleaning

Success! You Shot a Duck, Now What?

Once you bagged your duck it is time to clean it. You should try to clean your ducks within 1-2 hours of shooting them (if this is legal in your area) to ensure that the meat is still fresh and does not have a chance to go bad before you get it into a cool area. If you are hunting in very cold temperatures you can wait a little longer; however, if you are hunting during the warm early season you should consider cleaning your birds shortly after they are shot, or at least putting them in a cooler.

Do note that some areas have regulations concerning the type of cleaning that can be done in the field as it might be necessary for authorities to be able to identify the type of bird you are carrying if you are stopped on the way home. You might have to take your duck home to complete the cleaning process so check the regulations for your area.

You will need a hunting knife, gloves (if you desire), water, Ziploc bags, plastic grocery bags (if using whole duck process), trash bag(s) (if you will take remains home with you vs. discarding on site), and a cooler with ice in order to complete this process. (Unless it is very cold out or you will be going right home and live very close to your hunting site, you should always bring a cooler with you even if you don't plan to clean the birds as you would need it in this case to carry the whole, uncleaned birds. You might even want to have a cooler that you dedicate specifically to this purpose as you probably wouldn't want to use it for anything else afterwards.)

NOTE: Make sure you check any duck meat that you will be eating for BBs and remove them before preparing for consumption!

Below are the steps to do the following tasks:

- De-Breasting
- Removing the legs and thighs
- Preparing using the whole duck method

Steps for De-Breasting the Duck

STEP 1: Lie the duck on its back.

STEP 2: Pluck all of the feathers off of the breast area of the duck.

STEP 3: After all breast feathers are removed, use a knife to cut a line in the skin between the two duck breasts, trying to stay on top of the breast bone. Cut very shallow to only cut through the skin, not deep enough to cut the meat.

STEP 4: Once you make the cut, use your thumbs to grab the skin and pull it away towards the wings. Do this gently to try to keep the skin in one piece on each side as you pull it away.

STEP 5: Continue pulling away the breast skin until you have the breast meat completely exposed.

STEP 6: Take your knife and use it to cut along one side of the breast bone between the meat and the bone keeping the knife blade firmly against the breast bone. While doing this use the other hand to gently pull the meat away from the bone. Repeat this for the other breast.

STEP 7: Set aside the remaining carcass for disposal unless you want to remove the legs. See below to remove the legs.

Eighty percent of the duck meat is in the breasts so many people just remove this and leave the rest of the meat behind (this is referred to as "breasting out" the duck). If you are just starting out this will be the easiest way to get most of the duck meat with very little work. If you also want to keep the leg and thigh meat follow the steps below.

Steps to Remove the Legs and Thighs

If you want to remove the legs and thighs to keep this meat follow these steps:

STEP 1: Pluck all of the feathers from the leg and thigh areas of the duck.

STEP 2: Use a knife to cut off the feet from the legs and set these aside for disposal.

STEP 3: Take your knife and cut above thigh area at the base of leg where it connects to the body to remove the leg with the thigh attached. Repeat this for the other leg and thigh.

Whole Duck Preparation

Duck Hunting Made Simple: 21 Steps to Duck Hunting Success

Follow these steps to take the entire duck home for cooking:

STEP 1: Pluck all of the feathers from the leg, thigh, chest, and back area of the duck.

STEP 2: Use a knife to cut off the duck's head at the base of the neck where it connects to the body and set this aside for disposal.

STEP 3: Use a knife to cut off the feet from the legs and set these aside for disposal.

STEP 4: Use a knife to cut off each of the duck's wings at the base where they connect to the body and set these aside for disposal.

STEP 5: Take your knife and cut off the tail at the base where it connects to the body and set this aside for disposal.

STEP 6: Reach into the tail area and grab the insides at the opening including the intestines and set this all aside for disposal. Save the gizzard if you plan to eat it.

STEP 7: Reach further in and pull out the heart and liver and set these aside for disposal unless you plan to eat them.

STEP 8: Run plenty of cold water through the inside and outside of the duck. Be sure you check the inside well to ensure all entrails are cleaned from the duck.

If completing this process in the field, place all of the meat you are keeping in Ziploc bags and put them in a cooler. In the case of "whole duck" preparation, put the intact bird in a plastic bag and put it in a cooler. Dispose of the remaining duck carcass or parts either by bagging them and taking them home for disposal or leaving them in a spot where they are somewhat hidden from human traffic. They will most likely be taken care of rather quickly by crows, hawks or other animals. If you are performing this process at home, refrigerate or freeze all meat immediately after completing the cleaning process.

Bonus #1 Accelerate Your Duck Hunting Success

Shorten Your Learning Curve with a Guide

Booking a duck hunting guide for one day is a great way to dramatically speed up learning in order to be successful with hunting ducks. Guides have expert knowledge of hunting techniques and even one guided trip can help you greatly.

What you can learn from a guide:

- Decoy setup
- Duck calling
- Good locations

Finding a Guide

There are several ways to find a hunting guide. I list several below.

Ways to find a guide:

- Google search
- Craigslist
- Guide-booking agent
- Outdoor expo

If you do a Google search for duck hunting guides in whatever area you are looking to hunt you will likely find several. Using a computer, another place you can look is Craigslist. Hunting guide agents are also common in the industry. Essentially, their role is to help connect hunters with hunting guides. Typically agents know which guides do good work. It is in their best interest to set you up with a good guide so you book through them again and refer others to use their service. Finally, you can attend an outdoor expo where you will be sure to find a guide that will take you hunting.

Cost to Hire a Guide

You can hire a guide at a reasonable rate and it will be well worth the expense for the amount of time and frustration you will save. In addition to rates often being reasonable this can be a great way to test out duck hunting before investing in all of the equipment required to later find out that you do not enjoy the sport. Depending on what type of guide you hire they may have a gun for you to use. This means that for a reasonable fee you can try all aspects of duck hunting prior to going all in.

Average rates:

- Half day: $80-$150 per person
- Full day: $90-$200 per person

Factors that typically impact the cost:

- Time of season (usually there are premium rates for opening weekend)
- Area being hunted
- Whether or not a group discount could apply

Bonus #2 Painting and Repairing Decoys

Save Money by Painting and Repairing Decoys

If you are like me and you enjoy hunting ducks but don't have a lot of money to spend on hunting supplies, then painting and repairing decoys is a great way to save money.

Reasons you should paint and repair your duck decoys:

- It can be a huge financial savings
- Beat up decoys are less effective
- You can purchase used decoys and refresh them with paint
- Personal satisfaction of using decoys that you painted

For many outdoor enthusiasts we truly love hunting but there is the challenge of funding our hobby. The costs can quickly add up with guns, clothing, gas, shells and decoys. By painting your decoys yourself you can significantly save money as opposed to buying new ones once your current set gets old.

You can also save money by purchasing used decoys and painting them to look new. When I first started my decoy spread I got a great deal on 24 decoys for $40; however, they were in pretty bad shape and needed to be re-painted. So I invested minimal time and money to do this on my own. I got great satisfaction knowing that I was able to trick the birds to land in my decoys with the decoys I painted myself.

There are plenty of resources to help you with painting your decoys. If you visit my website at www.decoypro.com there are videos that provide you step-by-step instructions on how to paint your decoys. You can also get free printable instructions if you prefer. I think that you will be surprised how easy it can be to accomplish this task, especially with these resources.

Final Words

Congratulations! You have taken your first step in becoming a successful duck hunter.

Make Sure to Enjoy Yourself
Remember that hunting is fun but also challenging. Regardless of the success you have be sure you enjoy the time you spend outdoors.

Practice Makes Perfect
Getting started with anything can be challenging at first. Think back to when you first started tying your shoes. At first it was difficult, but after time it became second nature. This can be the same with duck hunting. The more you do it, the better you will get.

Make Progress Every Day
Using the steps learned in this book will help improve your duck hunting skills. I encourage you to make some type of progress each day of the season. Keep reading books, following hunting blogs and watching YouTube videos. Six months from now you will be surprised how far you have come by spending time learning more about duck hunting each day.

Want to Learn More?
Visit my website at decoypro.com

Made in the USA
Lexington, KY
29 March 2017